G'day, Ya Legends! Welcome to the Aussie Slang Safari!

Crikey, mate! You'v  f a read! This little beauty access pass to the w baffling world of A -blue local or a clueless visitor trying to someone just called you a "drongo," this guide has got you covered like sunscreen on Bondi Beach.

Aussies have a way with words that turns the mundane into the magical. Here, a simple breakfast becomes a "brekkie," a quick nap is a "snooze," and your best mate might casually call you a "bogan" (but only if they really like you). It's a language rich in humor, wit, and a fair bit of laziness—why use a full word when you can chop it in half and add an "-ie" at the end?

Inside these pages, you'll learn how to decode a chat at the pub, survive a barbie with the rellies, and maybe even discover what in the bloody hell a "galah" has to do with being a fool. Don't worry—this book isn't here to judge your lack of Aussie know-how. We're here to take you on a laugh-filled journey through the linguistic bushland, where every word has a story and every story has a laugh.

So, chuck on your thongs (the ones for your feet, not the beach), grab a cuppa, and dive in. You'll be yabbering like a true Aussie legend in no time. And remember, if it all gets a bit confusing, just smile, nod, and say, "Too right, mate!" You'll fit right in.

Welcome to Straya, where the slang is weird, and the laughs are plenty. Let's get cracking!

TABLE OF CONTENT

- *A* 5
- *B* 8
- *C* 12
- *D* 16
- *F* 23
- *G* 27
- *H* 31
- *I* 35
- *J* 39
- *K* 43
- *L* 47
- *M* 51
- *N* 55
- *O* 60
- *P* 64
- *R* 69
- *S* 73
- *T* 77
- *U* 81
- *V* 86
- *W* 90
- *X* 94

Y..*98*

Z...*102*

Where is your next travel ?

SCAN THE QR

Get the Slang Dictionary Collection

Slang Dictionaries Availables:

- French
- Mexican
- German
- Italian
- Colombian
- Many More...

A

1. **Arvo**
   Example: "Let's catch up this arvo."
   Translation: "Let's meet this afternoon."
   Explanation: Short for "afternoon," used casually.
2. **Aussie**
   Example: "I'm proud to be an Aussie."
   Translation: "I'm proud to be an Australian."
   Explanation: A common term for an Australian person.
3. **Ambo**
   Example: "The ambo arrived quickly after the accident."
   Translation: "The ambulance arrived quickly after the accident."
   Explanation: Slang for "ambulance" or "ambulance worker."
4. **Aggro**
   Example: "Don't get so aggro about it."
   Translation: "Don't get so aggressive about it."
   Explanation: Means angry or aggressive.
5. **Avo**
   Example: "I had smashed avo for breakfast."
   Translation: "I had smashed avocado for breakfast."
   Explanation: Short for "avocado," often used in food contexts.
6. **Ankle biter**
   Example: "The ankle biters are running around the yard."
   Translation: "The children are running around the yard."
   Explanation: A playful term for small children.

7. **Aussie salute**
   Example: "He's doing the Aussie salute out there."
   Translation: "He's waving away flies out there."
   Explanation: Refers to the hand motion used to swat flies away.
8. **Ace**
   Example: "That performance was ace!"
   Translation: "That performance was excellent!"
   Explanation: Means something great or excellent.
9. **Akubra**
   Example: "He tipped his Akubra as a greeting."
   Translation: "He tipped his wide-brimmed hat as a greeting."
   Explanation: A brand of iconic Australian hats.
10. **Aggie**
    Example: "The Aggies are blooming beautifully this year."
    Translation: "The Agapanthus flowers are blooming beautifully this year."
    Explanation: Short for the flower "Agapanthus."
11. **Aerial ping-pong**
    Example: "Are you watching aerial ping-pong tonight?"
    Translation: "Are you watching Australian Rules Football tonight?"
    Explanation: A light-hearted nickname for Australian football.
12. **Amber fluid**
    Example: "He enjoys a bit of amber fluid after work."

Translation: "He enjoys a beer after work."
Explanation: Refers to beer due to its color.

13. **Av-a-go-yer-mug**
    Example: "Av-a-go-yer-mug, kick the ball!"
    Translation: "Have a try, you fool, kick the ball!"
    Explanation: Encourages someone to make an attempt, often in sports.

14. **Aussie battler**
    Example: "He's a real Aussie battler, working two jobs to get by."
    Translation: "He's a hardworking Australian struggling to make ends meet."
    Explanation: Refers to an everyday Australian overcoming hardships.

15. **Ambo's lot**
    Example: "It was the ambo's lot to deal with the big crash."
    Translation: "It was the ambulance crew's task to handle the big crash."
    Explanation: Describes the duty or responsibility of ambulance staff.

16. **Aussie rules**
    Example: "I'm a huge fan of Aussie rules."
    Translation: "I'm a huge fan of Australian Rules Football."
    Explanation: The sport native to Australia.

17. **Away with the pixies**
    Example: "She's away with the pixies today."
    Translation: "She's daydreaming today."
    Explanation: Refers to someone being distracted or daydreaming.

18. **Avocado toast brigade**
    Example: "The avocado toast brigade loves the new café."

Translation: "The trendy crowd loves the new café."

Explanation: A humorous term for millennials or trendy people.

19. **Air con**

    Example: "Turn on the air con; it's boiling in here."

    Translation: "Turn on the air conditioning; it's very hot in here."

    Explanation: Short for air conditioner.

20. **Aunty**

    Example: "Aunty is airing the cricket match today."

    Translation: "The ABC channel is airing the cricket match today."

    Explanation: A nickname for the Australian Broadcasting Corporation (ABC).

B

1. **Barbie**
   Example: "We're having a barbie this weekend."
   Translation: "We're having a barbecue this weekend."
   Explanation: A widely used term for a barbecue.
2. **Bogan**
   Example: "He's such a bogan with his flannel shirt."
   Translation: "He's such a working-class person with his flannel shirt."
   Explanation: Refers to someone perceived as unsophisticated or from the working class.
3. **Bottler**
   Example: "That new car is an absolute bottler!"
   Translation: "That new car is absolutely fantastic!"
   Explanation: Describes something excellent or outstanding.
4. **Bonza**
   Example: "What a bonza idea to have a picnic!"
   Translation: "What a great idea to have a picnic!"
   Explanation: An older term meaning great or excellent.
5. **Brolly**
   Example: "Don't forget your brolly; it's raining outside."
   Translation: "Don't forget your umbrella; it's raining outside."
   Explanation: Short for "umbrella."

6. **Bloody oath**
   Example: "Bloody oath, I'll be there!"
   Translation: "Absolutely, I'll be there!"
   Explanation: A strong affirmation, meaning "absolutely" or "definitely."
7. **Bushie**
   Example: "He's a true bushie; he loves the outback."
   Translation: "He's a true bush person; he loves the rural areas."
   Explanation: Refers to someone who lives or thrives in the Australian bush.
8. **Bottle-o**
   Example: "I'll stop by the bottle-o to grab some drinks."
   Translation: "I'll stop by the liquor store to grab some drinks."
   Explanation: A liquor store or bottle shop.
9. **Bloke**
   Example: "That bloke over there looks familiar."
   Translation: "That man over there looks familiar."
   Explanation: A casual term for a man or guy.
10. **Beauty**
    Example: "You fixed it? Beauty, mate!"
    Translation: "You fixed it? Awesome, mate!"
    Explanation: An exclamation expressing delight or approval.
11. **Bush tucker**
    Example: "We learned about bush tucker on our trip."
    Translation: "We learned about traditional native Australian food on our trip."
    Explanation: Refers to food native to the

Australian bush, often used by Indigenous Australians.

12. **Brekkie**
    Example: "Let's grab some brekkie before heading out."
    Translation: "Let's grab some breakfast before heading out."
    Explanation: A casual term for breakfast.

13. **Bludger**
    Example: "That guy is such a bludger, never does any work."
    Translation: "That guy is so lazy, he never does any work."
    Explanation: Refers to someone lazy or unwilling to work.

14. **Boofhead**
    Example: "Don't be such a boofhead!"
    Translation: "Don't be so silly or clumsy!"
    Explanation: A playful insult meaning a silly or awkward person.

15. **Bickie**
    Example: "Would you like a bickie with your tea?"
    Translation: "Would you like a biscuit (cookie) with your tea?"
    Explanation: Short for "biscuit," often referring to cookies.

16. **Buckley's chance**
    Example: "You've got Buckley's chance of winning that game."
    Translation: "You've got no chance of winning that game."
    Explanation: Means having very little or no chance of success.

17. **Bush bash**
    Example: "We're going on a bush bash this weekend."
    Translation: "We're going on an adventure through the bush this weekend."
    Explanation: Refers to a journey or party in the bush.
18. **Back of Bourke**
    Example: "That place is out the back of Bourke."
    Translation: "That place is extremely remote."
    Explanation: Refers to a very distant or remote location.
19. **Big smoke**
    Example: "I'm heading to the big smoke for work."
    Translation: "I'm heading to the city for work."
    Explanation: Refers to a major city.
20. **Bathers**
    Example: "Don't forget your bathers for the beach."
    Translation: "Don't forget your swimsuit for the beach."
    Explanation: Common term for swimwear.

C

1. **Cuppa**
   Example: "Come in for a cuppa."
   Translation: "Come in for a cup of tea or coffee."
   Explanation: Refers to a hot beverage, typically tea or coffee.

2. **Chook**
   Example: "The chooks are clucking in the yard."
   Translation: "The chickens are clucking in the yard."
   Explanation: A common term for a chicken.

3. **Crikey**
   Example: "Crikey, that's a huge spider!"
   Translation: "Wow, that's a huge spider!"
   Explanation: An exclamation of surprise or amazement.

4. **Crook**
   Example: "I feel a bit crook today."
   Translation: "I feel a bit unwell today."
   Explanation: Means feeling sick or ill.

5. **Cobber**
   Example: "G'day cobber, how's it going?"
   Translation: "Hello mate, how's it going?"
   Explanation: An old-fashioned term for a close friend or mate.

6. **Cactus**
   Example: "The car's cactus; it won't start."
   Translation: "The car's broken; it won't start."
   Explanation: Means something is broken or not functioning.

7. **Chewie**
   Example: "Got any chewie?"
   Translation: "Do you have any chewing gum?"
   Explanation: Slang for chewing gum.
8. **Coldie**
   Example: "Let's grab a coldie after work."
   Translation: "Let's grab a cold beer after work."
   Explanation: Refers to a cold beer.
9. **Clucky**
   Example: "She's feeling clucky around the baby."
   Translation: "She's feeling maternal around the baby."
   Explanation: Describes someone feeling broody or maternal.
10. **Cozzie**
    Example: "Don't forget your cozzie for the pool."
    Translation: "Don't forget your swimsuit for the pool."
    Explanation: A term for swimwear, common in some regions.
11. **Chrissie**
    Example: "What are your plans for Chrissie this year?"
    Translation: "What are your plans for Christmas this year?"
    Explanation: Short for "Christmas."
12. **Chuck a sickie**
    Example: "I might chuck a sickie tomorrow."
    Translation: "I might take a day off work pretending to be sick tomorrow."
    Explanation: Refers to taking a sick day when not actually unwell.

13. **Chuck a U-ey**
Example: "We missed the turn; chuck a U-ey."
Translation: "We missed the turn; make a U-turn."
Explanation: Means to perform a U-turn while driving.

14. **Cut snake**
Example: "He was mad as a cut snake."
Translation: "He was very angry."
Explanation: Refers to someone who is extremely angry or erratic.

15. **Corker**
Example: "That was a corker of a game!"
Translation: "That was an excellent game!"
Explanation: Describes something excellent or outstanding.

16. **Coldie holder**
Example: "Grab me a coldie holder for my beer."
Translation: "Grab me a stubby holder for my beer."
Explanation: Refers to an insulated sleeve for keeping drinks cold.

17. **Crack onto**
Example: "I think he's trying to crack onto her."
Translation: "I think he's trying to flirt with her."
Explanation: Means to flirt or make romantic advances.

18. **Cark it**
Example: "The old fridge finally carked it."
Translation: "The old fridge finally broke down."
Explanation: Means to die or stop working.

19. **Crow eater**
Example: "He's a crow eater from Adelaide."
Translation: "He's a person from Adelaide, South Australia."
Explanation: A nickname for South Australians.

20. **Catch ya later**
Example: "I'm off now; catch ya later!"
Translation: "I'm leaving now; see you later!"
Explanation: A casual way of saying goodbye.

D

1. **Daks**
   Example: "Your daks are on backwards, mate!"
   Translation: "Your trousers are on backwards, mate!"
   Explanation: Refers to trousers or pants.
2. **Drongo**
   Example: "Don't be such a drongo!"
   Translation: "Don't be such an idiot!"
   Explanation: A term used to describe a fool or simpleton.
3. **Dunny**
   Example: "Where's the dunny around here?"
   Translation: "Where's the toilet around here?"
   Explanation: A casual term for a toilet.
4. **Dag**
   Example: "He's a bit of a dag, but we love him."
   Translation: "He's a bit unfashionable, but we love him."
   Explanation: A playful insult meaning someone unfashionable or a bit odd.
5. **Dinky-di**
   Example: "He's a dinky-di Aussie."
   Translation: "He's a genuine Aussie."
   Explanation: Means authentic or genuine.
6. **Dropbear**
   Example: "Watch out for dropbears in the bush!"
   Translation: "Watch out for fictional predatory koalas in the bush!"
   Explanation: A humorous myth used to scare tourists.

7. **Doona**
   Example: "It's cold; I'm staying under the doona."
   Translation: "It's cold; I'm staying under the duvet."
   Explanation: Refers to a duvet or comforter.
8. **Deckie**
   Example: "He works as a deckie on a fishing boat."
   Translation: "He works as a deckhand on a fishing boat."
   Explanation: A term for a deckhand.
9. **Deadset**
   Example: "Deadset, that's the best pie I've ever had!"
   Translation: "Seriously, that's the best pie I've ever had!"
   Explanation: Means genuinely or seriously.
10. **Devo**
    Example: "I'm devo about missing the game."
    Translation: "I'm devastated about missing the game."
    Explanation: Short for devastated, meaning upset.
11. **Dog's breakfast**
    Example: "Your room looks like a dog's breakfast!"
    Translation: "Your room is a complete mess!"
    Explanation: Refers to something messy or disorganized.
12. **Dagwood dog**
    Example: "Grab a Dagwood dog from the show."
    Translation: "Grab a corndog from the fair."

Explanation: Australian term for a battered and fried hotdog on a stick.

13. **Digger**
Example: "My grandpa was a digger in the war."
Translation: "My grandpa was a soldier in the war."
Explanation: Refers to an Australian soldier, especially from WWI or WWII.

14. **Dollop**
Example: "Just add a dollop of cream to the pie."
Translation: "Just add a spoonful of cream to the pie."
Explanation: Refers to a generous portion, often of a soft substance.

15. **Drum**
Example: "What's the drum on the new job?"
Translation: "What's the news on the new job?"
Explanation: Means news, information, or gossip.

16. **Dusty**
Example: "I'm feeling a bit dusty after last night."
Translation: "I'm feeling a bit hungover after last night."
Explanation: Describes the feeling of being hungover.

17. **Dunny diver**
Example: "I wouldn't want to be a dunny diver!"
Translation: "I wouldn't want to clean out portable toilets!"

Explanation: Refers to someone who cleans septic tanks or toilets.

18. **Dob in**
Example: "She dobbed him in to the teacher."
Translation: "She reported him to the teacher."
Explanation: Means to tattle or report someone's actions.

19. **Dead horse**
Example: "Want some dead horse on your pie?"
Translation: "Want some tomato sauce (ketchup) on your pie?"
Explanation: Rhyming slang for tomato sauce.

20. **Dry as a dead dingo's donger**
Example: "The land out here is as dry as a dead dingo's donger."
Translation: "The land out here is extremely dry."
Explanation: A humorous way to say something is very dry or arid.

E

1. **Esky**
   Example: "Grab the beers from the esky."
   Translation: "Grab the beers from the cooler."
   Explanation: A portable cooler used for keeping drinks or food cold.

2. **Earbasher**
   Example: "He's a real earbasher when he starts talking politics."
   Translation: "He talks non-stop when he starts talking about politics."
   Explanation: Refers to someone who talks excessively or at length.

3. **Exy**
   Example: "That restaurant is a bit exy, isn't it?"
   Translation: "That restaurant is a bit expensive, isn't it?"
   Explanation: Short for expensive.

4. **Emu-bob**
   Example: "We had to do an emu-bob to clean the park."
   Translation: "We had to pick up litter in the park."
   Explanation: Refers to cleaning up by picking up rubbish, likened to the foraging motion of an emu.

5. **Earbash**
   Example: "She'll earbash you if you're late again."
   Translation: "She'll scold you if you're late again."
   Explanation: To criticize or lecture someone at length.

6. **Epic**
   Example: "That surf session was epic!"
   Translation: "That surf session was amazing!"
   Explanation: Used to describe something incredible or outstanding.
7. **Elbow grease**
   Example: "Put some elbow grease into scrubbing that pan."
   Translation: "Use some effort to scrub that pan."
   Explanation: A phrase meaning hard physical effort.
8. **Enzedder**
   Example: "He's an Enzedder, so he loves his rugby."
   Translation: "He's a New Zealander, so he loves his rugby."
   Explanation: Aussie slang for a person from New Zealand.
9. **Every man and his dog**
   Example: "Every man and his dog was at the beach today."
   Translation: "It was very crowded at the beach today."
   Explanation: Means a large number of people.
10. **Eighty-clicks**
    Example: "The next petrol station is eighty-clicks away."
    Translation: "The next petrol station is eighty kilometers away."
    Explanation: Refers to kilometers, often in a rural context.
11. **Eat like a horse**
    Example: "He eats like a horse after footy practice."

Translation: "He eats a lot after football practice."
Explanation: Refers to someone with a large appetite.

12. **Egg flip**
Example: "Mum made me an egg flip for breakfast."
Translation: "Mum made me an egg-based drink for breakfast."
Explanation: A milkshake-like drink with raw eggs.

13. **End of the line**
Example: "Looks like we've hit the end of the line for repairs."
Translation: "It seems there's nothing more we can do to fix it."
Explanation: Refers to the conclusion of something.

14. **Esky dive**
Example: "He did an esky dive to grab the last beer."
Translation: "He rummaged through the cooler to grab the last beer."
Explanation: Jokingly refers to diving into a cooler for a drink.

15. **Easy as**
Example: "Fixing that tap was easy as."
Translation: "Fixing that tap was very simple."
Explanation: Indicates something was very easy, often with no further comparison.

16. **Eel through**
Example: "He managed to eel through the crowd to the front."
Translation: "He managed to wriggle through the crowd to the front."

Explanation: Means moving deftly or sneakily through a tight space.

17. **Egg on**
Example: "They egged him on to do the stunt."
Translation: "They encouraged him to do the stunt."
Explanation: Refers to inciting or urging someone to do something.

18. **Earth-shattering**
Example: "The news wasn't exactly earth-shattering."
Translation: "The news wasn't particularly surprising or important."
Explanation: Refers to something major or significant, often used ironically.

19. **Eyes like a hawk**
Example: "She's got eyes like a hawk; she spotted the mistake instantly."
Translation: "She's very observant; she spotted the mistake instantly."
Explanation: Describes someone who notices small details.

20. **Esky lid**
Example: "He hit the waves with an esky lid as a makeshift board."
Translation: "He used a cooler lid as an improvised surfboard."
Explanation: Refers to using unconventional equipment, often for fun.

F

1. **Fair dinkum**
   Example: "Are you fair dinkum about quitting your job?"
   Translation: "Are you serious about quitting your job?"
   Explanation: Means genuine, authentic, or serious.

2. **Footy**
   Example: "We're heading to the footy this weekend."
   Translation: "We're going to the football game this weekend."
   Explanation: Refers to Australian Rules Football or rugby, depending on the region.

3. **Flat out like a lizard drinking**
   Example: "I've been flat out like a lizard drinking all week."
   Translation: "I've been extremely busy all week."
   Explanation: Humorous way of saying very busy.

4. **Fair go**
   Example: "Everyone deserves a fair go."
   Translation: "Everyone deserves an equal chance."
   Explanation: Refers to fairness and equal opportunities.

5. **Furphy**
   Example: "That's just a furphy; don't believe it."
   Translation: "That's just a rumor; don't believe it."

Explanation: Refers to a false or misleading story.
6. **Fang it**
   Example: "We're running late; fang it!"
   Translation: "We're running late; drive fast!"
   Explanation: Means to go fast, usually when driving.
7. **Fair crack of the whip**
   Example: "Give me a fair crack of the whip, will you?"
   Translation: "Give me a fair chance, will you?"
   Explanation: Refers to giving someone a fair opportunity.
8. **Flanno**
   Example: "He's wearing his favorite flanno today."
   Translation: "He's wearing his favorite flannel shirt today."
   Explanation: Refers to a flannel shirt, often associated with casual or rural attire.
9. **Frothy**
   Example: "Let's grab a frothy at the pub."
   Translation: "Let's grab a beer at the pub."
   Explanation: A casual term for a beer.
10. **Facey**
    Example: "Did you see that post on Facey?"
    Translation: "Did you see that post on Facebook?"
    Explanation: A shortened nickname for Facebook.
11. **Fair suck of the sav**
    Example: "Fair suck of the sav, mate, let me explain!"
    Translation: "Give me a fair chance, mate, let me explain!"

Explanation: An idiomatic way of asking for a fair opportunity to speak or act.

12. **Figjam**
Example: "He's a bit of a FIGJAM, isn't he?"
Translation: "He's a bit full of himself, isn't he?"
Explanation: Acronym for "F*** I'm Good, Just Ask Me," describing someone arrogant.

13. **Flick**
Example: "I'll flick you a text later."
Translation: "I'll send you a text later."
Explanation: Means to send or quickly give something.

14. **Flat chat**
Example: "We're flat chat getting this done by Friday."
Translation: "We're working as hard as possible to get this done by Friday."
Explanation: Means to be very busy or going at full speed.

15. **Franger**
Example: "Don't forget to bring some frangers."
Translation: "Don't forget to bring some condoms."
Explanation: Informal term for condoms.

16. **Full as a goog**
Example: "I'm full as a goog after that meal."
Translation: "I'm very full after that meal."
Explanation: Means extremely full, often after eating or drinking.

17. **Flick the bird**
Example: "He flicked the bird at the driver who cut him off."
Translation: "He made a rude gesture at the

driver who cut him off."
Explanation: Refers to raising the middle finger in a rude gesture.

18. **Fly wire**

    Example: "Close the fly wire, or the mozzies will get in."
    Translation: "Close the screen door, or the mosquitoes will get in."
    Explanation: Refers to a screen door.

19. **Foot falcon**

    Example: "We'll have to take the foot falcon to the shops."
    Translation: "We'll have to walk to the shops."
    Explanation: A humorous term for walking.

20. **Flog**

    Example: "Stop being such a flog, mate."
    Translation: "Stop being such an idiot, mate."
    Explanation: Used to describe someone annoying or foolish.

G

1. **G'day**
   Example: "G'day, mate! How's it going?"
   Translation: "Hello, mate! How are you?"
   Explanation: A quintessential Australian greeting.

2. **Garbo**
   Example: "The garbo comes early on Tuesdays."
   Translation: "The garbage collector comes early on Tuesdays."
   Explanation: Refers to a garbage collector.

3. **Good on ya**
   Example: "Good on ya for helping out!"
   Translation: "Well done for helping out!"
   Explanation: Used to express praise or appreciation.

4. **Grog**
   Example: "Bring some grog to the barbecue."
   Translation: "Bring some alcohol to the barbecue."
   Explanation: A term for alcohol, especially beer.

5. **Greenie**
   Example: "She's a greenie, always talking about saving the environment."
   Translation: "She's an environmentalist, always talking about saving the environment."
   Explanation: Refers to an environmentally conscious person.

6. **Galah**
   Example: "Don't act like a galah!"
   Translation: "Don't act like a fool!"

Explanation: A bird known for its loud behavior, used to describe someone silly.

7. **Goldie**
Example: "We're heading to the Goldie this weekend."
Translation: "We're heading to the Gold Coast this weekend."
Explanation: A nickname for the Gold Coast in Queensland.

8. **Gone walkabout**
Example: "He's gone walkabout in the middle of the job."
Translation: "He's disappeared in the middle of the job."
Explanation: Originally referring to Indigenous Australian practices, now used to describe someone wandering or disappearing.

9. **Grouse**
Example: "That new bike is grouse!"
Translation: "That new bike is excellent!"
Explanation: Means great, excellent, or cool.

10. **Gutful**
Example: "I've had a gutful of this noise!"
Translation: "I've had enough of this noise!"
Explanation: Indicates being fed up with something.

11. **Give it a burl**
Example: "I've never tried surfing, but I'll give it a burl."
Translation: "I've never tried surfing, but I'll give it a go."
Explanation: Means to attempt something.

12. **Gnarly**
Example: "That was a gnarly wave, mate!"
Translation: "That was an impressive wave,

mate!"
Explanation: Used to describe something extreme or impressive, often in surfing.

13. **Get stuffed**
Example: "If you don't like it, get stuffed!"
Translation: "If you don't like it, go away!"
Explanation: A blunt way of telling someone off.

14. **Go bush**
Example: "We're going bush for the weekend."
Translation: "We're going to the countryside for the weekend."
Explanation: Means to head out into rural or remote areas.

15. **Giggle water**
Example: "Care for some giggle water?"
Translation: "Care for some alcoholic drinks?"
Explanation: A playful term for alcohol.

16. **Gone troppo**
Example: "After months in the heat, he's gone troppo."
Translation: "After months in the heat, he's gone a bit crazy."
Explanation: Refers to someone acting oddly, often due to tropical heat.

17. **Gibber**
Example: "That's just a load of gibber."
Translation: "That's just a load of nonsense."
Explanation: Refers to senseless or unintelligible talk.

18. **Goanna**
Example: "We spotted a massive goanna near the campsite."
Translation: "We spotted a massive lizard near

the campsite."
Explanation: A large lizard native to Australia.

19. **Give us a bell**
    Example: "Give us a bell when you're free."
    Translation: "Call me when you're free."
    Explanation: Means to make a phone call.

20. **Get your gear off**
    Example: "It's so hot, I'm about to get my gear off."
    Translation: "It's so hot, I'm about to take my clothes off."
    Explanation: A casual way to say remove clothing.

H

1. **Heaps**
   Example: "Thanks heaps for your help!"
   Translation: "Thanks a lot for your help!"
   Explanation: Means a large amount or a lot of something.
2. **Hooroo**
   Example: "Hooroo, mate! See you tomorrow."
   Translation: "Goodbye, mate! See you tomorrow."
   Explanation: A casual Australian way of saying goodbye.
3. **Hard yakka**
   Example: "Building this fence is hard yakka."
   Translation: "Building this fence is hard work."
   Explanation: Refers to hard work or effort.
4. **Hit the frog and toad**
   Example: "It's getting late, time to hit the frog and toad."
   Translation: "It's getting late, time to hit the road."
   Explanation: A playful rhyming slang for leaving or traveling.
5. **Havachat**
   Example: "We'll havachat over coffee."
   Translation: "We'll have a conversation over coffee."
   Explanation: Means to have a chat or talk.
6. **Hoon**
   Example: "The hoons were doing burnouts in the car park."
   Translation: "The reckless drivers were doing

stunts in the car park."
Explanation: Refers to someone driving recklessly or dangerously.

7. **Hot as**
Example: "It's hot as today, better stay inside."
Translation: "It's extremely hot today, better stay inside."
Explanation: An abbreviation emphasizing extreme heat.

8. **Hooch**
Example: "He got in trouble for growing hooch in his backyard."
Translation: "He got in trouble for growing marijuana in his backyard."
Explanation: Informal term for marijuana.

9. **Hubby**
Example: "My hubby is cooking dinner tonight."
Translation: "My husband is cooking dinner tonight."
Explanation: A casual term for husband.

10. **Have a go**
Example: "Stop complaining and have a go!"
Translation: "Stop complaining and try it!"
Explanation: Encourages someone to make an attempt.

11. **Hill's hoist**
Example: "Hang your clothes on the Hill's hoist."
Translation: "Hang your clothes on the rotary clothesline."
Explanation: A traditional Australian outdoor clothesline.

12. **Hottie**
Example: "Chuck a hottie in the bed; it's

freezing tonight."
Translation: "Put a hot water bottle in the bed; it's freezing tonight."
Explanation: Refers to a hot water bottle.

13. **Hard case**
Example: "He's such a hard case; he always makes me laugh."
Translation: "He's so funny; he always makes me laugh."
Explanation: Refers to someone who is humorous or quirky.

14. **Half-arsed**
Example: "Don't do a half-arsed job on the painting."
Translation: "Don't do a poor-quality or incomplete job on the painting."
Explanation: Describes something done poorly or without full effort.

15. **Hung like a drover's dog**
Example: "He's bragging again, saying he's hung like a drover's dog."
Translation: "He's bragging again about his physical endowment."
Explanation: A humorous, often crude, phrase referring to a man's anatomy.

16. **Hot under the collar**
Example: "He got hot under the collar when they called him lazy."
Translation: "He got angry when they called him lazy."
Explanation: Means to get angry or flustered.

17. **Hoodie**
Example: "Grab your hoodie; it's chilly outside."
Translation: "Grab your hooded sweatshirt; it's

chilly outside."
Explanation: A casual term for a hooded sweatshirt.

18. **Hit the sack**
Example: "I'm knackered; time to hit the sack."
Translation: "I'm exhausted; time to go to bed."
Explanation: Refers to going to bed.

19. **Hard yakka gear**
Example: "I bought some new hard yakka gear for work."
Translation: "I bought some new durable work clothes."
Explanation: Refers to tough, practical work clothing.

20. **Head like a dropped pie**
Example: "He's got a head like a dropped pie, but he's a good bloke."
Translation: "He's not very good-looking, but he's a nice guy."
Explanation: A humorous and self-deprecating phrase about appearance.

I

1. **Iffy**
   Example: "This meat smells a bit iffy."
   Translation: "This meat smells a bit suspicious."
   Explanation: Means uncertain, questionable, or not quite right.

2. **Icy pole**
   Example: "It's so hot; I could go for an icy pole."
   Translation: "It's so hot; I could go for a popsicle."
   Explanation: Australian term for a frozen ice treat on a stick.

3. **Idiot box**
   Example: "He's been glued to the idiot box all day."
   Translation: "He's been watching the television all day."
   Explanation: A playful, derogatory term for the television.

4. **In for a penny, in for a pound**
   Example: "We've already started, so we're in for a penny, in for a pound."
   Translation: "We've already started, so we might as well fully commit."
   Explanation: Refers to committing fully to a task or situation.

5. **It'll be right**
   Example: "Don't worry about the mess; it'll be right."
   Translation: "Don't worry about the mess; everything will be fine."

Explanation: Means things will work out okay in the end.

6. **Ironman**
   Example: "He's training for the Ironman this summer."
   Translation: "He's training for the triathlon this summer."
   Explanation: Refers to a competitive athletic event involving swimming, cycling, and running.
7. **Ice-block**
   Example: "I'll grab an ice-block from the freezer."
   Translation: "I'll grab a frozen treat from the freezer."
   Explanation: Another term for a popsicle or frozen dessert.
8. **In a tick**
   Example: "I'll be there in a tick."
   Translation: "I'll be there in a moment."
   Explanation: Means a very short amount of time.
9. **I reckon**
   Example: "I reckon it's going to rain soon."
   Translation: "I think it's going to rain soon."
   Explanation: Means to believe or think something.
10. **In strife**
    Example: "He's in strife for missing his deadline."
    Translation: "He's in trouble for missing his deadline."
    Explanation: Means to be in trouble or difficulty.

11. **Info sesh**
    Example: "There's an info sesh about the new project tomorrow."
    Translation: "There's an informational session about the new project tomorrow."
    Explanation: Shortened term for an information session.
12. **I'm not here to f*** spiders****
    Example: "Hurry up, mate; I'm not here to f*** spiders!"
    Translation: "Hurry up, mate; I'm here to get things done!"
    Explanation: A cheeky way of saying you're serious about doing something.
13. **Indie**
    Example: "She loves listening to indie music."
    Translation: "She loves listening to independent music."
    Explanation: Refers to independent or alternative styles, often music or films.
14. **Inner West**
    Example: "He's moving to the Inner West of Sydney."
    Translation: "He's moving to the inner western suburbs of Sydney."
    Explanation: Refers to a specific suburban region in Sydney.
15. **In the doghouse**
    Example: "He's in the doghouse for forgetting their anniversary."
    Translation: "He's in trouble for forgetting their anniversary."
    Explanation: Means to be in trouble, usually with a partner or authority figure.

16. Icy cold one
Example: "Let's crack open an icy cold one."
Translation: "Let's open a cold beer."
Explanation: Refers to a cold beverage, usually beer.

17. Irish handshake
Example: "He gave me an Irish handshake and disappeared."
Translation: "He gave me some money and disappeared."
Explanation: A humorous term for handing over money.

18. In the nuddy
Example: "He ran down the beach in the nuddy."
Translation: "He ran down the beach naked."
Explanation: Means being nude or naked.

19. It's your shout
Example: "You got the last round; it's your shout this time."
Translation: "You got the last round; it's your turn to pay this time."
Explanation: Refers to taking turns paying, especially for drinks.

20. Islander
Example: "She's an Islander from the Torres Strait."
Translation: "She's a person from the Torres Strait Islands."
Explanation: Refers to people from Pacific Islands or Torres Strait Islands.

J

1. **Jackaroo**
   Example: "He's working as a jackaroo on a cattle station."
   Translation: "He's working as a trainee on a cattle station."
   Explanation: A male trainee working on a sheep or cattle station.
2. **Jillaroo**
   Example: "She's a jillaroo learning the ropes on the farm."
   Translation: "She's a female trainee learning the ropes on the farm."
   Explanation: The female equivalent of a jackaroo.
3. **Joey**
   Example: "Look at that joey in its mother's pouch!"
   Translation: "Look at that baby kangaroo in its mother's pouch!"
   Explanation: Refers to a baby kangaroo.
4. **Jocks**
   Example: "I need to wash my jocks."
   Translation: "I need to wash my underwear."
   Explanation: A casual term for men's underwear.
5. **Juice**
   Example: "The car's out of juice; we need petrol."
   Translation: "The car's out of fuel; we need petrol."
   Explanation: Refers to fuel or power.
6. **Jumbuck**
   Example: "Waltzing Matilda mentions a

jumbuck."
Translation: "Waltzing Matilda mentions a sheep."
Explanation: A traditional term for sheep, used in Australian bush poetry.

7. **Jumbly**
Example: "The shop was all jumbly after the sale."
Translation: "The shop was all messy and disorganized after the sale."
Explanation: Describes something chaotic or mixed up.

8. **Jug**
Example: "Put the jug on for a cuppa."
Translation: "Boil the kettle for a cup of tea."
Explanation: Refers to an electric kettle.

9. **Jumper**
Example: "Grab a jumper; it's cold outside."
Translation: "Grab a sweater; it's cold outside."
Explanation: An Australian term for a sweater or pullover.

10. **Jaffles**
Example: "Let's make jaffles for lunch."
Translation: "Let's make toasted sandwiches for lunch."
Explanation: Refers to sandwiches toasted in a jaffle iron.

11. **Journo**
Example: "The journo wrote an article about the festival."
Translation: "The journalist wrote an article about the festival."
Explanation: A shortened term for a journalist.

12. **Jack of it**
    Example: "I'm jack of it; let's leave."
    Translation: "I'm tired of it; let's leave."
    Explanation: Means being fed up or tired of something.
13. **Jiggery-pokery**
    Example: "There's some jiggery-pokery going on with those numbers."
    Translation: "There's some trickery or deceit going on with those numbers."
    Explanation: Refers to dishonest or suspicious behavior.
14. **Jimmy Dunks**
    Example: "He ordered a Jimmy Dunks at the pub."
    Translation: "He ordered a glass of rum at the pub."
    Explanation: Rhyming slang for rum and coke.
15. **Jumbuck stew**
    Example: "We had jumbuck stew by the campfire."
    Translation: "We had lamb stew by the campfire."
    Explanation: Refers to a stew made with lamb or mutton.
16. **Jackaroo hat**
    Example: "He bought a jackaroo hat for the outback trip."
    Translation: "He bought a cowboy-style hat for the outback trip."
    Explanation: A wide-brimmed hat typically worn by outback workers.
17. **Junk mail**
    Example: "The letterbox is full of junk mail again."

Translation: "The letterbox is full of unsolicited advertisements again."
Explanation: Refers to unrequested promotional material delivered by mail.

18. **Juvie**
    Example: "He ended up in juvie after the fight."
    Translation: "He ended up in juvenile detention after the fight."
    Explanation: Short for juvenile detention or youth jail.

19. **Jumpy as a roo**
    Example: "She's jumpy as a roo before the exam."
    Translation: "She's very nervous before the exam."
    Explanation: Refers to someone feeling nervous or jumpy, like a kangaroo.

20. **Jackaroo boots**
    Example: "He's wearing his jackaroo boots to the rodeo."
    Translation: "He's wearing his cowboy boots to the rodeo."
    Explanation: Sturdy boots typically worn by jackaroos or outback workers.

K

1. **Kangaroo court**
   Example: "That meeting was a kangaroo court; no one was listening to the facts."
   Translation: "That meeting was unfair and biased; no one was listening to the facts."
   Explanation: A mock or biased court where decisions are made without fair judgment.

2. **Knee-high to a grasshopper**
   Example: "She's grown so much, but she was knee-high to a grasshopper not long ago!"
   Translation: "She's grown so much, but she was very small not long ago!"
   Explanation: Refers to someone or something very small, typically used when talking about children.

3. **Kanga**
   Example: "We had a kanga for lunch yesterday."
   Translation: "We had kangaroo meat for lunch yesterday."
   Explanation: A casual term for kangaroo, often referring to its meat.

4. **Knackered**
   Example: "I'm absolutely knackered after that hike."
   Translation: "I'm absolutely exhausted after that hike."
   Explanation: Means very tired or worn out.

5. **Kookaburra**
   Example: "The kookaburra was laughing in the tree this morning."
   Translation: "The kookaburra bird was making

its distinctive laughing sound in the tree this morning."
Explanation: Refers to the iconic Australian bird known for its unique laugh-like call.

6. **Knockback**
Example: "He got a knockback from the job interview."
Translation: "He was rejected from the job interview."
Explanation: Refers to rejection, often in a job or relationship context.

7. **Kiwi**
Example: "He's a Kiwi, born and raised in New Zealand."
Translation: "He's from New Zealand."
Explanation: A term for a person from New Zealand.

8. **Knee-slapping**
Example: "That comedian's jokes were knee-slapping funny."
Translation: "That comedian's jokes were very funny."
Explanation: Refers to something so funny that it makes you slap your knee in laughter.

9. **Kangaroo pouch**
Example: "She put the baby in the kangaroo pouch wrap to carry him."
Translation: "She put the baby in a baby carrier wrap."
Explanation: Refers to a baby carrier, likened to the pouch of a kangaroo.

10. **Keen as mustard**
Example: "She's keen as mustard to join us on the trip."
Translation: "She's very eager to join us on the

trip."
Explanation: Means very enthusiastic or eager.
11. **Knickers in a twist**
    Example: "Don't get your knickers in a twist over something so small."
    Translation: "Don't get upset over something trivial."
    Explanation: Refers to becoming unnecessarily upset or anxious.
12. **Kiss and tell**
    Example: "She's the type who loves to kiss and tell."
    Translation: "She's the type who shares details about her personal life or relationships."
    Explanation: Refers to someone who reveals private details about their romantic or personal life.
13. **Kook**
    Example: "He's a bit of a kook, always saying strange things."
    Translation: "He's a bit eccentric, always saying strange things."
    Explanation: Refers to a quirky or eccentric person.
14. **Kangaroo hop**
    Example: "We had to do a kangaroo hop to get to the car."
    Translation: "We had to jump like a kangaroo to get to the car."
    Explanation: Refers to hopping or jumping, like a kangaroo.
15. **Kick the bucket**
    Example: "He finally kicked the bucket after a long illness."
    Translation: "He passed away after a long

illness."
Explanation: A euphemism for dying.

16. Knuckle down
Example: "It's time to knuckle down and get this project finished."
Translation: "It's time to focus and finish this project."
Explanation: Refers to applying oneself seriously to a task.

17. Kettled
Example: "The police kettled the protestors at the rally."
Translation: "The police confined the protestors to a small area."
Explanation: Refers to trapping or confining a group of people in a specific area.

18. Keep your shirt on
Example: "Keep your shirt on, mate! We'll get there on time."
Translation: "Calm down, mate! We'll get there on time."
Explanation: Tells someone to remain calm or patient.

19. Kicking on
Example: "Are you kicking on after the party?"
Translation: "Are you continuing the night after the party?"
Explanation: Refers to continuing an activity, often partying or socializing.

20. Killer
Example: "That was a killer performance at the concert."
Translation: "That was an amazing performance at the concert."

Explanation: Used to describe something outstanding or impressive.

L

1. **Larrikin**
   Example: "He's a real larrikin, always joking around."
   Translation: "He's a playful and mischievous person, always joking around."
   Explanation: Refers to someone who is mischievous, playful, and enjoys causing harmless trouble.
2. **Lash**
   Example: "Let's have a lash at this new bar tonight."
   Translation: "Let's have a go at this new bar tonight."
   Explanation: Means to try or attempt something, especially something fun or adventurous.
3. **Lolly**
   Example: "He gave me a lolly for my birthday."
   Translation: "He gave me a candy for my birthday."
   Explanation: Australian term for a piece of candy or sweet.
4. **Loon**
   Example: "That guy's a bit of a loon."
   Translation: "That guy's a bit crazy or eccentric."
   Explanation: Refers to someone who behaves in a strange or crazy manner.
5. **Lob**
   Example: "I'll just lob this in the bin."
   Translation: "I'll just throw this in the bin."

Explanation: To throw or toss something, often casually.

6. **Larrikin spirit**
   Example: "She's full of the larrikin spirit, always having fun."
   Translation: "She's always playful and fun-loving."
   Explanation: Refers to a carefree, cheeky, and playful attitude or behavior.

7. **Lag**
   Example: "Don't lag behind; we're going for a run."
   Translation: "Don't fall behind; we're going for a run."
   Explanation: To fall behind, or to delay in joining or moving forward with a group.

8. **Lounge room**
   Example: "We watched the game in the lounge room."
   Translation: "We watched the game in the living room."
   Explanation: Another term for the living room or sitting room in a house.

9. **Long neck**
   Example: "I'll grab a long neck from the fridge."
   Translation: "I'll grab a bottle of beer from the fridge."
   Explanation: Refers to a long bottle of beer, typically 750ml.

10. **Livid**
    Example: "She was livid when she found out what happened."
    Translation: "She was extremely angry when

she found out what happened."
Explanation: Means very angry or enraged.

11. **Lazy daisy**

    Example: "Stop being a lazy daisy and help with the dishes!"
    Translation: "Stop being so lazy and help with the dishes!"
    Explanation: A playful way to call someone lazy or unmotivated.

12. **Lingo**

    Example: "He's picking up the Aussie lingo pretty quickly."
    Translation: "He's picking up the Australian slang pretty quickly."
    Explanation: Refers to the language or dialect, often slang or jargon.

13. **Lick of paint**

    Example: "The house just needs a lick of paint to look new again."
    Translation: "The house just needs a fresh coat of paint to look new again."
    Explanation: Refers to a quick or light touch-up, often in terms of painting or cleaning.

14. **Land of the long weekend**

    Example: "I'm heading to the land of the long weekend for a camping trip."
    Translation: "I'm heading to a place where long weekends are common, for a camping trip."
    Explanation: Refers to a place or situation where long weekends are frequently enjoyed.

15. **Lamb**

    Example: "We're having lamb chops for dinner."
    Translation: "We're having lamb chops for

dinner."
Explanation: Refers to the meat of a young sheep, commonly used in Australian cooking.

16. **Lollies**
    Example: "The kids were excited to get their hands on some lollies."
    Translation: "The kids were excited to get their hands on some candy."
    Explanation: Plural for sweets or candies.

17. **Loving it**
    Example: "He's loving it at the new job."
    Translation: "He's really enjoying his new job."
    Explanation: A phrase used to express that someone is thoroughly enjoying an experience.

18. **Low key**
    Example: "We're keeping it low key this weekend, just a quiet barbecue."
    Translation: "We're keeping it simple and relaxed this weekend, just a quiet barbecue."
    Explanation: Means to keep something understated, relaxed, or not overly extravagant.

19. **Lynx effect**
    Example: "He's got the Lynx effect going on, everyone's staring at him."
    Translation: "He's got that strong, attractive smell, and everyone's noticing him."
    Explanation: Refers to the strong scent from the Lynx brand of body sprays, often associated with attracting attention.

20. **Lager**
    Example: "I'll have a cold lager, thanks."
    Translation: "I'll have a cold beer, thanks."
    Explanation: Refers to a type of beer, specifically a pale lager.

M

1. **Maccas**
   Example: "Let's grab some food from Maccas on the way home."
   Translation: "Let's grab some food from McDonald's on the way home."
   Explanation: A popular Aussie nickname for McDonald's.
2. **Mongrel**
   Example: "He's a tough mongrel, don't mess with him."
   Translation: "He's a tough guy, don't mess with him."
   Explanation: Can refer to a tough or unruly person, but can also be used as an insult.
3. **Mate**
   Example: "How's it going, mate?"
   Translation: "How's it going, friend?"
   Explanation: A term used for a friend or buddy. It's one of the most common expressions in Australian English.
4. **Munted**
   Example: "I'm feeling munted after that party."
   Translation: "I'm feeling really worn out or drunk after that party."
   Explanation: Means exhausted, often after drinking or partying, or something that is broken or ruined.
5. **Mad as a cut snake**
   Example: "He was mad as a cut snake when he found out."
   Translation: "He was furious when he found out."

Explanation: Refers to someone who is very angry or upset.

6. **Mozzie**
Example: "Make sure you put on some spray, the mozzies are out tonight."
Translation: "Make sure you put on some insect repellent, the mosquitoes are out tonight."
Explanation: A colloquial term for mosquitoes.

7. **Moolah**
Example: "I need to make some moolah to pay the bills."
Translation: "I need to make some money to pay the bills."
Explanation: A casual term for money.

8. **Maggie**
Example: "I'll see you in the morning, Maggie."
Translation: "I'll see you in the morning, mate."
Explanation: An affectionate or informal shortening of "mate" (though less common than "mate").

9. **Mind the gap**
Example: "Mind the gap when you step off the train."
Translation: "Be careful of the space between the train and platform."
Explanation: A reminder to watch out for potential hazards, especially gaps.

10. **Monkey's uncle**
Example: "Well, I'll be a monkey's uncle!"
Translation: "Well, I can't believe it!"
Explanation: An exclamation of surprise or disbelief.

11. **Macca's run**
    Example: "Let's do a Macca's run and get some burgers."
    Translation: "Let's go to McDonald's and get some burgers."
    Explanation: Refers to going to McDonald's to grab food.
12. **Mud map**
    Example: "I'll give you a mud map of where the party is."
    Translation: "I'll give you a rough map of where the party is."
    Explanation: A simple or rough map, often drawn by hand.
13. **Moolah**
    Example: "He's got plenty of moolah from his new job."
    Translation: "He's got plenty of money from his new job."
    Explanation: Slang for money.
14. **Main drag**
    Example: "The shops are on the main drag of town."
    Translation: "The shops are on the main street of town."
    Explanation: Refers to the main street or central area of a town.
15. **Milko**
    Example: "The milko came by with the fresh milk."
    Translation: "The milkman came by with the fresh milk."
    Explanation: Short for milkman, who delivers milk to homes.

16. **Meltdown**
Example: "She had a meltdown when she couldn't find her keys."
Translation: "She had an emotional breakdown when she couldn't find her keys."
Explanation: Refers to a situation where someone becomes overly emotional or stressed.

17. **Mob**
Example: "We're meeting up with the mob at the pub."
Translation: "We're meeting up with the group of friends at the pub."
Explanation: A group of people, often referring to friends or acquaintances.

18. **Mooch**
Example: "He's always mooching off others for food."
Translation: "He's always scrounging food from others."
Explanation: To scrounge or beg, typically for food or favors.

19. **Moolah**
Example: "She's been making some serious moolah with her business."
Translation: "She's been making a lot of money with her business."
Explanation: Refers to money, often in a casual context.

20. **Mong**
Example: "Don't be a mong and start that argument."
Translation: "Don't be an idiot and start that argument."
Explanation: A derogatory term for a foolish or lazy person.

N

1. **No worries**
   Example: "Thanks for helping me out!"
   Translation: "No worries, happy to help!"
   Explanation: A very common phrase meaning "it's not a problem" or "no need to thank me."
2. **Noodle**
   Example: "I'm feeling like a noodle for dinner."
   Translation: "I'm feeling like having noodles for dinner."
   Explanation: Refers to noodles, a popular food item in Australia.
3. **Nark**
   Example: "Stop being a nark and just enjoy the party."
   Translation: "Stop being a grumpy person and just enjoy the party."
   Explanation: Refers to someone who is irritable or complaining.
4. **Nick**
   Example: "He got nicked for speeding."
   Translation: "He got arrested for speeding."
   Explanation: To get "nicked" means to be caught or arrested by the police.
5. **Nuts**
   Example: "That's absolutely nuts!"
   Translation: "That's completely crazy!"
   Explanation: Means something is insane, crazy, or outrageous.
6. **Napper**
   Example: "I'm just going for a napper, I'll be back in a bit."
   Translation: "I'm just going for a nap, I'll be

back soon."
Explanation: A casual term for a nap or short sleep.

7. **Ned**
Example: "He's a bit of a ned, always getting into trouble."
Translation: "He's a bit of a troublemaker, always causing problems."
Explanation: Refers to a person who is often involved in anti-social behavior, similar to "chav" in British slang.

8. **Nanna nap**
Example: "I'm having a nanna nap before we go out."
Translation: "I'm having a short nap before we go out."
Explanation: A short afternoon nap, often used to describe elderly people but can be used by anyone.

9. **Nude**
Example: "I'm going to the beach for a nude swim."
Translation: "I'm going to the beach for a swim without clothes (naked)."
Explanation: Informally refers to being naked, often used in contexts of swimming or sunbathing.

10. **Not on**
Example: "That behaviour is not on!"
Translation: "That behaviour is unacceptable!"
Explanation: Refers to something that is not acceptable or not appropriate.

11. **Nana**
Example: "My nana loves to bake cakes."
Translation: "My grandmother loves to bake

cakes."
Explanation: A common term for one's grandmother.

12. **Noodle around**
Example: "I was just noodling around on my guitar."
Translation: "I was just playing around on my guitar."
Explanation: To play or tinker with something, usually in a carefree manner.

13. **Nifty**
Example: "That's a nifty trick you've got there!"
Translation: "That's a clever trick you've got there!"
Explanation: Refers to something clever, skillful, or handy.

14. **Numbats**
Example: "We spotted some numbat at the zoo."
Translation: "We spotted some marsupials called numbats at the zoo."
Explanation: Refers to a small, nocturnal Australian marsupial, known for its striped appearance.

15. **Nanna's blanket**
Example: "I've been using nanna's blanket while watching TV."
Translation: "I've been using my grandmother's blanket while watching TV."
Explanation: A term for a comfortable, often homemade blanket, typically associated with coziness.

16. **Nosey parker**
Example: "Stop being a nosey parker and mind your own business."

Translation: "Stop being so curious and mind your own business."
Explanation: Refers to someone who is overly curious about other people's affairs.

17. **Narky**
Example: "Don't get narky with me, I was only joking."
Translation: "Don't get irritated with me, I was only joking."
Explanation: Means irritable or grumpy.

18. **Not the sharpest tool in the shed**
Example: "He's not the sharpest tool in the shed, but he means well."
Translation: "He's not very intelligent, but he has good intentions."
Explanation: A humorous way of saying someone is not very bright.

19. **Nitty gritty**
Example: "Let's get down to the nitty gritty and talk about the budget."
Translation: "Let's focus on the important details and talk about the budget."
Explanation: Refers to the most important or basic details of something.

20. **Noodle**
Example: "I'm just noodling my way through this project."
Translation: "I'm working through this project in a relaxed way."
Explanation: Refers to working or thinking through something casually.

O

1. **Off chops**

   Example: "That party was off chops, best night ever!"

   Translation: "That party was amazing, the best night ever!"

   Explanation: A term meaning something is excellent or very exciting.

2. **Oi**

   Example: "Oi, what are you doing?"

   Translation: "Hey, what are you doing?"

   Explanation: A casual and direct way to get someone's attention.

3. **Onya**

   Example: "You got the job? Onya, mate!"

   Translation: "You got the job? Good on you, mate!"

   Explanation: A casual way to say "good on you" or "well done."

4. **Oldies**

   Example: "I'm going to visit the oldies this weekend."

   Translation: "I'm going to visit my parents this weekend."

   Explanation: Informal term for one's parents, often used affectionately.

5. **Outback**

   Example: "We're going on a road trip to the outback."

   Translation: "We're going on a road trip to the remote, rural parts of Australia."

   Explanation: Refers to the vast, remote, and sparsely populated areas of Australia.

6. **Ocker**
   Example: "He's a bit of an ocker, always talking about footy."
   Translation: "He's very Australian, always talking about footy."
   Explanation: Refers to a stereotype of a very Aussie, sometimes rough, or unsophisticated person.
7. **Over the moon**
   Example: "I was over the moon when I got the promotion."
   Translation: "I was extremely happy when I got the promotion."
   Explanation: Refers to being extremely happy or pleased about something.
8. **On the piss**
   Example: "We were out on the piss last night."
   Translation: "We were out drinking last night."
   Explanation: A colloquial term for going out drinking alcohol, especially in excess.
9. **Off to the flicks**
   Example: "We're off to the flicks to see the new movie."
   Translation: "We're going to the movies to see the new film."
   Explanation: A casual way of saying "going to the cinema."
10. **Over it**
    Example: "I'm totally over it, I don't want to hear about it anymore."
    Translation: "I'm tired of it, I don't want to hear about it anymore."
    Explanation: A way of expressing that you're tired or fed up with something.

11. **On the go**
    Example: "I've been on the go all day."
    Translation: "I've been busy all day, constantly moving around."
    Explanation: Refers to being busy and active, not taking a break.
12. **Off like a frog in a sock**
    Example: "When the bell rang, the kids were off like a frog in a sock."
    Translation: "When the bell rang, the kids ran off quickly and energetically."
    Explanation: Refers to something moving or happening very quickly, often in an energetic way.
13. **Out of pocket**
    Example: "I'm a bit out of pocket after the trip."
    Translation: "I'm short on money after the trip."
    Explanation: Refers to spending money or being in debt, typically after an expense.
14. **On the nose**
    Example: "The milk's gone off, it's really on the nose."
    Translation: "The milk's gone bad, it smells awful."
    Explanation: Refers to something smelling bad, often used to describe spoiled food.
15. **Out of the blue**
    Example: "He called me out of the blue after years."
    Translation: "He called me unexpectedly after years."
    Explanation: Refers to something happening unexpectedly or without warning.

16. **Only in it for the lollies**
 Example: "He's only in it for the lollies, not the hard work."
 Translation: "He's only interested in the rewards or easy parts, not the effort."
 Explanation: Refers to someone who is only interested in the benefits or rewards, not the work.

17. **Out of sorts**
 Example: "I'm feeling a bit out of sorts today."
 Translation: "I'm feeling a bit off or unwell today."
 Explanation: Refers to feeling unwell, tired, or not quite right.

18. **On your bike**
 Example: "He told me to get on my bike and leave."
 Translation: "He told me to leave."
 Explanation: A slang way of telling someone to leave or go away.

19. **On the up and up**
 Example: "Things are on the up and up at work."
 Translation: "Things are improving or going well at work."
 Explanation: Refers to something that is improving, becoming more successful, or growing.

20. **One for the road**
 Example: "Let's have one for the road before we leave."
 Translation: "Let's have one last drink before we leave."
 Explanation: A phrase used to suggest having one final drink before parting ways.

P

1. **Pissed**
   Example: "He's completely pissed after the party."
   Translation: "He's completely drunk after the party."
   Explanation: Refers to being drunk or intoxicated, commonly used in Australia.

2. **Piker**
   Example: "Don't be a piker, come to the party!"
   Translation: "Don't be a coward, come to the party!"
   Explanation: Refers to someone who backs out of something at the last minute or is afraid to participate.

3. **Pull your head in**
   Example: "Pull your head in, you're going too far."
   Translation: "Stop overreacting or behaving inappropriately."
   Explanation: A warning to someone to stop being rude, arrogant, or overstepping boundaries.

4. **Pash**
   Example: "They had a big pash at the party."
   Translation: "They had a passionate kiss at the party."
   Explanation: Informal term for kissing, often in a romantic or passionate way.

5. **Pav**
   Example: "Mum's making a pav for dessert."
   Translation: "Mum's making a pavlova for dessert."
   Explanation: Shortened term for pavlova, a

popular Australian dessert made of meringue, fruit, and cream.
6. **Prawn**
   Example: "I'll grab a few prawns for the BBQ."
   Translation: "I'll grab a few shrimp for the BBQ."
   Explanation: Refers to shrimp in Australian English, especially when grilling or preparing food.
7. **Pooch**
   Example: "I've got to walk the pooch before dinner."
   Translation: "I've got to walk the dog before dinner."
   Explanation: A colloquial term for a dog.
8. **Pass me by**
   Example: "That whole event just passed me by."
   Translation: "I completely missed that event."
   Explanation: Refers to something that happens without being noticed or experienced.
9. **Pre-drinks**
   Example: "We're having pre-drinks at my place before heading to the club."
   Translation: "We're having drinks at my place before going to the club."
   Explanation: Refers to the drinks consumed before going out to a party or bar.
10. **Pot**
    Example: "I'll have a pot of beer, thanks."
    Translation: "I'll have a small glass of beer, thanks."
    Explanation: A common term for a small-sized beer (usually around 285ml) in Australia.

11. **Pillock**
    Example: "Stop being a pillock and help me with this!"
    Translation: "Stop being a fool and help me with this!"
    Explanation: A derogatory term for a silly or foolish person.
12. **Pick up**
    Example: "I'll pick you up at 7 for dinner."
    Translation: "I'll come by and get you at 7 for dinner."
    Explanation: Refers to collecting someone or something, typically with a car.
13. **Put the boot in**
    Example: "He really put the boot in when he criticized her presentation."
    Translation: "He was very harsh when he criticized her presentation."
    Explanation: To criticize or attack someone or something, often in a harsh or unfair way.
14. **Poo**
    Example: "I need to take a poo before we leave."
    Translation: "I need to use the bathroom before we leave."
    Explanation: A childish or casual term for feces, often used in informal or light-hearted conversations.
15. **Pineapple**
    Example: "That's as Aussie as a pineapple on a pizza!"
    Translation: "That's very Australian, just like having pineapple on pizza."
    Explanation: Pineapple is often associated

with Australian culture, particularly in the context of pizza.

16. **Put out**
Example: "I didn't mean to put her out, she looked really upset."
Translation: "I didn't mean to upset her, she looked really sad."
Explanation: Refers to causing someone to feel upset, bothered, or inconvenienced.

17. **Pip**
Example: "That guy's got a pip in his step today!"
Translation: "That guy seems very cheerful today!"
Explanation: A term to describe someone who's energetic, excited, or happy.

18. **Peckish**
Example: "I'm feeling a bit peckish, do you have any snacks?"
Translation: "I'm feeling a bit hungry, do you have any snacks?"
Explanation: A light term for being slightly hungry.

19. **Pony**
Example: "Can you lend me a pony?"
Translation: "Can you lend me $25?"
Explanation: "Pony" is Australian slang for $25, often used in betting contexts.

20. **Pash rash**
Example: "He had pash rash after their make-out session."
Translation: "He had irritation or a rash on his face after their kiss."
Explanation: The redness or irritation that can occur on the skin after a passionate kiss.

Q

1. **Quokka**
   Example: "We saw a quokka when we were on Rottnest Island."
   Translation: "We saw a small marsupial when we were on Rottnest Island."
   Explanation: A small, friendly marsupial found in Australia, especially on Rottnest Island, often known for its photogenic smile.

2. **Quick smart**
   Example: "Get over here quick smart, we need to leave!"
   Translation: "Get over here quickly, we need to leave!"
   Explanation: An expression used to tell someone to do something quickly.

3. **Quid**
   Example: "That'll cost you 20 quid."
   Translation: "That'll cost you 20 dollars."
   Explanation: Slang for money, often referring to Australian dollars or just any general currency.

4. **Quaint**
   Example: "That little cottage is quite quaint, isn't it?"
   Translation: "That little cottage is very charming and old-fashioned, isn't it?"
   Explanation: Refers to something that is charming, old-fashioned, and picturesque.

5. **Quash**
   Example: "The authorities quashed the protest before it got out of hand."
   Translation: "The authorities stopped the

protest before it escalated."
Explanation: To suppress, stop, or put an end to something, especially in a forceful or official manner.

6. **Quid pro quo**
   Example: "I helped him with his work, and he gave me a quid pro quo by buying me dinner."
   Translation: "I helped him with his work, and in return, he bought me dinner."
   Explanation: A Latin phrase that means "something for something" or an exchange of favors.

7. **Quick stick**
   Example: "We need to move quick stick, the train's about to leave!"
   Translation: "We need to move quickly, the train's about to leave!"
   Explanation: A casual way to say "quickly" or "immediately."

8. **Quirky**
   Example: "He has a quirky sense of humor."
   Translation: "He has an unusual or eccentric sense of humor."
   Explanation: Refers to something that is odd, unusual, or charmingly different.

9. **Quidditch**
   Example: "They played a game of Quidditch, but with a frisbee instead of a ball."
   Translation: "They played a modified version of the fictional sport from *Harry Potter*, using a frisbee."
   Explanation: A reference to the fictional sport from *Harry Potter* but sometimes used humorously to describe an energetic or chaotic game.

10. **Queue jump**
Example: "Don't even think about queue jumping, everyone's waiting their turn."
Translation: "Don't think about skipping the line, everyone's waiting their turn."
Explanation: Refers to skipping ahead in a line, usually in a rude or unfair manner.

11. **Quill**
Example: "He wrote the letter with a quill and ink."
Translation: "He wrote the letter with a pen and ink."
Explanation: Refers to an old-fashioned pen made from a bird's feather, often used in historical contexts.

12. **Quake**
Example: "The house shook during the earthquake; it was a real quake!"
Translation: "The house shook during the earthquake; it was very intense!"
Explanation: Refers to an earthquake, or metaphorically, a situation that causes significant disruption or shock.

13. **Quad bike**
Example: "We went for a ride on the quad bikes in the desert."
Translation: "We went for a ride on the all-terrain vehicles in the desert."
Explanation: A four-wheeled motorbike designed for off-road riding.

14. **Quaint little town**
Example: "We stayed in a quaint little town on our road trip."
Translation: "We stayed in a charming and picturesque little town on our road trip."

Explanation: Refers to a small, charming, and often old-fashioned town.

15. **Quince**
Example: "She made a quince jam to serve with the cheese."
Translation: "She made a jam from quince fruit to serve with the cheese."
Explanation: A type of fruit, sometimes used in jams and preserves.

16. **Quack**
Example: "The doctor's a bit of a quack, so I'm getting a second opinion."
Translation: "The doctor is unqualified or not very skilled, so I'm getting a second opinion."
Explanation: A slang term for an unqualified or fraudulent doctor, or anyone offering questionable medical advice.

17. **Quilted**
Example: "I'm feeling cozy in my quilted jacket today."
Translation: "I'm feeling warm and comfy in my quilted jacket today."
Explanation: Refers to something that's padded, often for warmth.

18. **Quick as a flash**
Example: "She fixed the problem quick as a flash."
Translation: "She fixed the problem very quickly."
Explanation: A way to describe something done very quickly or rapidly.

19. **Quarterback**
Example: "He's the quarterback of the team, leading everyone to victory."
Translation: "He's the leader of the team,

guiding everyone to success."
Explanation: Borrowed from American football, used to refer to a leader or someone in control of a situation.

20. **Quickfire**

    Example: "We had a quickfire round of trivia at the pub."
    Translation: "We had a fast-paced round of trivia at the pub."
    Explanation: Refers to something done rapidly or in quick succession.

R

1. **Ripper**
   Example: "That was a ripper of a game last night!"
   Translation: "That was an excellent game last night!"
   Explanation: Used to describe something that is fantastic, great, or excellent.
2. **Rough as guts**
   Example: "He's as rough as guts, always causing trouble."
   Translation: "He's very rough, tough, and often unpleasant."
   Explanation: Refers to someone or something that is coarse, uncaring, or rough around the edges.
3. **Rack off**
   Example: "Rack off, mate, I'm trying to get some work done!"
   Translation: "Go away, mate, I'm trying to get some work done!"
   Explanation: A more forceful way of telling someone to leave or get lost.
4. **Rodeo**
   Example: "It's going to be a bit of a rodeo getting this project finished on time."
   Translation: "It's going to be a bit chaotic getting this project finished on time."
   Explanation: Refers to something wild, chaotic, or difficult, often related to work or a challenging situation.
5. **Root**
   Example: "They were caught rooting in the

back of the pub."
Translation: "They were caught making out or engaging in sexual activity."
Explanation: Slang for sexual intercourse or to make out, used in a more casual sense.

6. **Ripper**
Example: "That was a ripper of a night!"
Translation: "That was a fantastic night!"
Explanation: A way to say something is excellent or impressive, often used for events or experiences.

7. **Round the twist**
Example: "I think he's gone round the twist, he's been acting really strange lately."
Translation: "I think he's lost his mind, he's been acting really strange lately."
Explanation: Refers to someone who is acting irrationally or seems a bit crazy.

8. **Red hot**
Example: "She's red hot right now after winning that award."
Translation: "She's extremely successful or popular right now after winning that award."
Explanation: Can refer to something that is very successful, popular, or in high demand.

9. **Rug up**
Example: "It's freezing outside, better rug up before you go out."
Translation: "It's cold outside, better bundle up before you go out."
Explanation: To dress warmly, usually in preparation for cold weather.

10. **Reckon**
Example: "I reckon we should head to the beach this weekend."

Translation: "I think we should head to the beach this weekend."
Explanation: Informal term for "think" or "believe."

11. **Rollover**
    Example: "The car did a rollover after losing control."
    Translation: "The car flipped over after losing control."
    Explanation: Refers to a car accident where the car turns over, or more generally, to something that turns over or changes drastically.

12. **Roast**
    Example: "You gave him a good roast in front of everyone!"
    Translation: "You really embarrassed him in front of everyone!"
    Explanation: Refers to teasing or mocking someone, usually in a playful but harsh way.

13. **Razzle**
    Example: "The nightclub was full of razzle, with lights and music everywhere."
    Translation: "The nightclub was full of excitement, with lights and music everywhere."
    Explanation: Refers to a showy or exciting display, often in the context of entertainment or flashy things.

14. **Reckless**
    Example: "His reckless driving caused a lot of damage."
    Translation: "His careless or dangerous driving caused a lot of damage."
    Explanation: Describes behavior that is reckless, dangerous, or irresponsible.

15. **Rattle the cage**
Example: "You're going to rattle the cage if you keep pushing like that."
Translation: "You're going to cause problems or stir things up if you keep pushing like that."
Explanation: Refers to creating trouble or causing a stir, often when someone challenges authority or the status quo.
16. **Rip-off**
Example: "That's a total rip-off! You're charging too much."
Translation: "That's a scam! You're charging too much."
Explanation: Refers to something that is overpriced or unfair, often implying that someone is being cheated.
17. **Rough it**
Example: "We had to rough it during the camping trip, no showers for days!"
Translation: "We had to endure a very basic or uncomfortable situation during the camping trip, with no showers for days!"
Explanation: To endure difficult or uncomfortable conditions, often in the context of camping or outdoor adventures.
18. **Rocker**
Example: "He's a real rocker, always playing in his band."
Translation: "He's a musician who plays in a band, especially a rock band."
Explanation: A term for someone who is part of a rock band or someone who enjoys rock music.
19. **Rough diamond**
Example: "She's a rough diamond—very blunt,

but kind-hearted."

Translation: "She's a person who may seem tough or blunt on the outside but is actually kind-hearted and valuable."

Explanation: Describes someone who has great potential or inner value but might come across as rough or unpolished on the surface.

20. **Reckon on**

    Example: "I reckon on going to the movies this weekend."

    Translation: "I plan on going to the movies this weekend."

    Explanation: An expression of intention or planning, often used in casual conversation.

S

1. **Sick**
   Example: "That new movie was sick!"
   Translation: "That new movie was amazing!"
   Explanation: Used to describe something that is extremely good or impressive.

2. **Stoked**
   Example: "I'm so stoked about the surf tomorrow!"
   Translation: "I'm really excited about the surf tomorrow!"
   Explanation: To be extremely happy or excited about something.

3. **Suss**
   Example: "That deal seems a bit suss to me."
   Translation: "That deal seems a bit suspicious to me."
   Explanation: Short for "suspect," meaning something that seems questionable or untrustworthy.

4. **Smoko**
   Example: "It's smoko time, mate!"
   Translation: "It's break time, mate!"
   Explanation: A break, especially for a smoke or a rest, commonly used in workplaces.

5. **She'll be right**
   Example: "Don't worry about it, she'll be right."
   Translation: "Don't worry about it, everything will be fine."
   Explanation: A phrase used to reassure someone that everything will be okay, even if it seems uncertain.

6. **Slab**
   Example: "Grab a slab of beer for the party."
   Translation: "Grab a case (usually 24 bottles) of beer for the party."
   Explanation: Refers to a carton or case of beer, commonly used in Australia.
7. **Shed**
   Example: "He's out in the shed working on his car."
   Translation: "He's out in the garage working on his car."
   Explanation: A small, usually outdoor building, often used for storage or work, like a garage.
8. **Shout**
   Example: "I'll shout you a drink at the pub."
   Translation: "I'll buy you a drink at the pub."
   Explanation: Used to say that you will buy something for someone, usually referring to drinks.
9. **Straya**
   Example: "G'day, mate! Welcome to Straya!"
   Translation: "Hello, mate! Welcome to Australia!"
   Explanation: An informal and affectionate way of referring to Australia.
10. **Strewth**
    Example: "Strewth, that was close!"
    Translation: "Wow, that was close!"
    Explanation: An exclamation used to express surprise or astonishment.
11. **Sook**
    Example: "Stop being such a sook and get back to work!"
    Translation: "Stop being so whiny and get back

to work!"

Explanation: Refers to someone who is being overly sensitive or acting like a baby.

12. **Spiffy**

    Example: "You look spiffy in that suit!"

    Translation: "You look very stylish in that suit!"

    Explanation: Used to describe something or someone that looks sharp, neat, or stylish.

13. **Shonky**

    Example: "That's a shonky business deal, I wouldn't trust it."

    Translation: "That's a dodgy business deal, I wouldn't trust it."

    Explanation: Describes something that is dishonest, fraudulent, or unreliable.

14. **Slosh**

    Example: "You sloshed your drink all over the carpet!"

    Translation: "You spilled your drink all over the carpet!"

    Explanation: To spill or slosh liquid carelessly, especially when it makes a mess.

15. **Sickie**

    Example: "I'm pulling a sickie tomorrow to catch up on sleep."

    Translation: "I'm taking a day off sick tomorrow to catch up on sleep."

    Explanation: A day off from work or school, often when someone isn't really sick but uses it as an excuse.

16. **Swag**

    Example: "We camped out with our swag under the stars."

    Translation: "We camped out with our

sleeping bags or portable beds under the stars."
Explanation: A portable bed or sleeping bag used for camping, commonly associated with outdoor adventures.

17. **Sanga**
    Example: "I'm hungry, I could go for a sanga."
    Translation: "I'm hungry, I could go for a sandwich."
    Explanation: A casual term for a sandwich.

18. **Squiz**
    Example: "Just give it a quick squiz, will ya?"
    Translation: "Just take a quick look at it, will you?"
    Explanation: A short way of saying "look" or "glance."

19. **Shirty**
    Example: "Don't get all shirty with me!"
    Translation: "Don't get angry or upset with me!"
    Explanation: Describes someone who is getting upset or annoyed, often in an easily irritated manner.

20. **Screwy**
    Example: "That guy's a bit screwy, don't trust him."
    Translation: "That guy's a bit crazy, don't trust him."
    Explanation: Refers to someone or something that is strange, odd, or not quite right.

T

1. **Tucker**
   Example: "Let's grab some tucker before we hit the road."
   Translation: "Let's grab some food before we hit the road."
   Explanation: Informal word for food, often used when talking about a meal or snack.
2. **Thongs**
   Example: "It's too hot for shoes, I'm wearing my thongs."
   Translation: "It's too hot for shoes, I'm wearing my flip-flops."
   Explanation: In Australia, "thongs" refer to flip-flops, the casual summer footwear.
3. **Tightarse**
   Example: "Don't be a tightarse and buy the first round!"
   Translation: "Don't be stingy and buy the first round!"
   Explanation: A term for someone who is overly cheap or stingy with money.
4. **True blue**
   Example: "He's a true blue Aussie, born and raised in the outback."
   Translation: "He's a genuine Aussie, born and raised in the outback."
   Explanation: Used to describe someone who is authentically Australian, or something that is truly Australian.
5. **Toke**
   Example: "He had a quick toke before heading to the party."

Translation: "He had a quick puff of marijuana before heading to the party."
Explanation: Refers to taking a hit or puff from a cigarette or a joint, particularly marijuana.

6. **Take the piss**
   Example: "He's just taking the piss out of you, don't take it seriously."
   Translation: "He's just joking with you, don't take it seriously."
   Explanation: To mock, tease, or make fun of someone.

7. **Tart up**
   Example: "She spent hours tarting up for the party."
   Translation: "She spent hours getting dressed up and looking good for the party."
   Explanation: Refers to someone making themselves look more attractive or putting effort into their appearance.

8. **Trolleyed**
   Example: "After a few drinks, he was completely trolleyed."
   Translation: "After a few drinks, he was completely drunk."
   Explanation: Slang for being extremely drunk or intoxicated.

9. **Tosser**
   Example: "What a tosser! He doesn't know what he's talking about."
   Translation: "What an idiot! He doesn't know what he's talking about."
   Explanation: A derogatory term used to refer to a fool, idiot, or jerk.

10. **Trackie daks**
    Example: "I'm just going to wear my trackie

daks to the shops."
Translation: "I'm just going to wear my sweatpants to the shops."
Explanation: A term for track pants or sweatpants, often worn casually at home.

11. **Take a squiz**
Example: "Take a squiz at this new car!"
Translation: "Take a look at this new car!"
Explanation: Refers to taking a quick look or glance at something.

12. **Tart**
Example: "She's a real tart, always flirting with everyone."
Translation: "She's a bit of a flirt, always trying to attract attention."
Explanation: A derogatory term for someone, usually a woman, who is considered overly flirtatious.

13. **Turn up like a shag on a rock**
Example: "She turned up like a shag on a rock to the meeting, completely unprepared."
Translation: "She turned up completely out of place or unprepared to the meeting."
Explanation: Refers to someone arriving in an awkward or inappropriate situation.

14. **Tuckshop**
Example: "I'll meet you at the tuckshop for lunch."
Translation: "I'll meet you at the cafeteria for lunch."
Explanation: A term for a school or workplace canteen or snack bar.

15. **Throw a wobbly**
Example: "He threw a wobbly when they cancelled the game."

Translation: "He threw a tantrum when they cancelled the game."
Explanation: Refers to someone becoming very upset, throwing a tantrum, or losing their temper.

16. **Tight as a drum**
Example: "That's tight as a drum, we don't have any more space!"
Translation: "That's packed tightly, we don't have any more space!"
Explanation: Refers to something that is tightly packed or very difficult to squeeze into.

17. **Tidy**
Example: "That's a tidy little car you've got there."
Translation: "That's a neat, well-maintained little car you've got there."
Explanation: Used to describe something that is neat, well-kept, or in good condition.

18. **Torch**
Example: "I had to use a torch to find my way out of the cave."
Translation: "I had to use a flashlight to find my way out of the cave."
Explanation: The Australian term for a flashlight.

19. **Throw a spanner in the works**
Example: "This new issue really threw a spanner in the works."
Translation: "This new issue really messed up our plans."
Explanation: Refers to causing a disruption or problem that interferes with a plan or process.

20. **Two bob each way**
Example: "He's playing two bob each way on

this bet."
Translation: "He's betting on both sides of the issue."
Explanation: Refers to trying to benefit from two opposing sides of a situation.

U

1. **Ute**
   Example: "I'll throw the gear in the back of the ute."
   Translation: "I'll throw the gear in the back of the pickup truck."
   Explanation: Short for "utility vehicle," referring to a pick-up truck with an open cargo area.

2. **Up for it**
   Example: "Are you up for a surf this afternoon?"
   Translation: "Are you willing to go for a surf this afternoon?"
   Explanation: Used to ask if someone is interested in doing something, or ready for an activity.

3. **U-turn**
   Example: "You missed the turn, make a U-turn at the next roundabout."
   Translation: "You missed the turn, make a turn in the opposite direction at the next roundabout."
   Explanation: A complete reversal in direction, typically used in reference to driving.

4. **Under the pump**
   Example: "I'm really under the pump with this deadline."
   Translation: "I'm under a lot of pressure to meet this deadline."
   Explanation: Refers to being under stress or pressure, especially when dealing with work or tasks.

5. **Up to no good**
   Example: "They look like they're up to no good."
   Translation: "They seem like they're planning trouble or mischief."
   Explanation: Used to describe someone who is behaving suspiciously or planning something dishonest.
6. **Unreal**
   Example: "The view from the top of the mountain was unreal!"
   Translation: "The view from the top of the mountain was amazing!"
   Explanation: Used to describe something that is extraordinarily good or impressive.
7. **Under the weather**
   Example: "I'm feeling a bit under the weather today."
   Translation: "I'm feeling a bit sick today."
   Explanation: Refers to feeling ill or unwell, often used casually.
8. **Up the duff**
   Example: "She's up the duff, she's expecting a baby."
   Translation: "She's pregnant, she's expecting a baby."
   Explanation: A slang term for being pregnant, often used humorously or informally.
9. **Up to scratch**
   Example: "I don't think his work is up to scratch."
   Translation: "I don't think his work is up to the required standard."
   Explanation: Refers to something meeting the expected or required standard.

10. **Used to it**
    Example: "You'll get used to the heat, don't worry."
    Translation: "You'll become accustomed to the heat, don't worry."
    Explanation: Refers to becoming accustomed to something over time, especially something initially challenging.
11. **Unrealistic**
    Example: "That's an unrealistic expectation for a weekend."
    Translation: "That's an unreasonable or impossible expectation for a weekend."
    Explanation: Refers to something that is not feasible or practical.
12. **Up in the air**
    Example: "The plans for the weekend are still up in the air."
    Translation: "The plans for the weekend are still undecided or uncertain."
    Explanation: Refers to something that is uncertain or undecided.
13. **Ugly mug**
    Example: "He's got a real ugly mug, doesn't he?"
    Translation: "He's got an unattractive face, doesn't he?"
    Explanation: A derogatory term referring to someone's unattractive appearance.
14. **Under wraps**
    Example: "Keep it under wraps until the big announcement."
    Translation: "Keep it secret until the big announcement."

Explanation: Refers to keeping something secret or hidden from others.

15. **Up the creek**
Example: "We're up the creek without a paddle here!"
Translation: "We're in big trouble and have no way out!"
Explanation: Used when someone is in a difficult situation without a clear solution.

16. **Up to speed**
Example: "We need to get everyone up to speed on the project."
Translation: "We need to update everyone on the progress of the project."
Explanation: Refers to ensuring that someone has the latest information about something.

17. **Ubiquitous**
Example: "Mobile phones are ubiquitous nowadays."
Translation: "Mobile phones are everywhere nowadays."
Explanation: Refers to something that is found everywhere or very common.

18. **Under the influence**
Example: "He was caught driving under the influence last night."
Translation: "He was caught driving while drunk or on drugs last night."
Explanation: Refers to being affected by alcohol or drugs, especially when engaging in activities like driving.

19. **Up for grabs**
Example: "The last ticket is up for grabs, who wants it?"
Translation: "The last ticket is available to be

taken, who wants it?"
Explanation: Refers to something that is available and up for taking, usually in a competitive context.

20. **Unbeaten track**
Example: "We're going off the beaten track for this holiday."
Translation: "We're going somewhere less touristy for this holiday."
Explanation: Refers to traveling or doing something in a less conventional or popular way, often in nature or adventure.

V

1. **Veg out**
    Example: "I'm just going to veg out on the couch tonight."
    Translation: "I'm just going to relax and do nothing on the couch tonight."
    Explanation: Refers to relaxing in a lazy manner, often while watching TV or doing little.

2. **Vibe**
    Example: "The vibe at the party was really chill."
    Translation: "The atmosphere at the party was really relaxed."
    Explanation: Refers to the general feeling or atmosphere of a place, event, or situation.

3. **Vino**
    Example: "Let's open a bottle of vino and have dinner."
    Translation: "Let's open a bottle of wine and have dinner."
    Explanation: Informal term for wine, commonly used in casual conversations.

4. **Veggie**
    Example: "I'm having a veggie stir-fry for lunch."
    Translation: "I'm having a vegetable stir-fry for lunch."
    Explanation: Short for vegetables, often used in a casual, everyday context.

5. **Vox pop**
    Example: "The news show did a vox pop to get people's opinions on the election."

Translation: "The news show did a public opinion interview to get people's thoughts on the election."
Explanation: Short for "voice of the people," referring to a survey or interview with the public.

6. **Vulnerable**
Example: "She felt vulnerable when her phone was stolen."
Translation: "She felt defenseless or exposed when her phone was stolen."
Explanation: Refers to feeling exposed, weak, or unprotected in a situation.

7. **Vocal**
Example: "He's very vocal about his political views."
Translation: "He openly expresses his political views."
Explanation: Used to describe someone who speaks their mind openly and clearly, especially on controversial topics.

8. **Vibe check**
Example: "Let's do a vibe check before we head to the party."
Translation: "Let's make sure the mood or atmosphere is right before we head to the party."
Explanation: Refers to assessing the general atmosphere or mood of a situation or event.

9. **Vigilante**
Example: "The local vigilantes keep an eye on the neighborhood."
Translation: "The local community members take matters into their own hands to protect the neighborhood."

Explanation: A person who takes the law into their own hands to protect their community or solve issues.

10. **Vapour**

    Example: "He's gone off in a vapour after that argument."

    Translation: "He's left suddenly, probably because of that argument."

    Explanation: Refers to someone disappearing or leaving in a rush, especially after a tense or dramatic moment.

11. **Vocal fry**

    Example: "She has that vocal fry when she talks, it's hard to listen to."

    Translation: "She speaks with a particular voice quality that sounds rough and strained."

    Explanation: Refers to a type of speech where the voice sounds creaky or raspy, usually at the end of sentences.

12. **Venture out**

    Example: "I'm not sure if I want to venture out in this weather."

    Translation: "I'm not sure if I want to go out in this weather."

    Explanation: Refers to going outside or taking a trip somewhere, especially when it's not ideal to do so.

13. **Vibe out**

    Example: "Let's vibe out and see where the night takes us."

    Translation: "Let's just go with the flow and see where the night leads."

    Explanation: Refers to going along with the mood or atmosphere and not planning anything specific.

14. **Vow to**
Example: "I vow to make this summer the best one yet!"
Translation: "I promise to make this summer the best one yet!"
Explanation: To make a serious promise or declaration to do something.

15. **Varnish**
Example: "The furniture is looking great after a coat of varnish."
Translation: "The furniture looks great after being coated with varnish."
Explanation: Refers to a finishing coat used on wood or furniture to enhance appearance or protect it.

16. **Vulture**
Example: "He's a bit of a vulture, always picking up leftovers."
Translation: "He's a bit opportunistic, always taking advantage of situations for his own benefit."
Explanation: Used to describe someone who takes advantage of others' misfortune or exploits opportunities selfishly.

17. **Vocal cords**
Example: "I lost my voice from shouting, my vocal cords are sore."
Translation: "I lost my voice from shouting, my throat is sore."
Explanation: Refers to the muscles in your throat that are responsible for making sound when you speak or sing.

18. **Vis a vis**
Example: "We need to discuss the situation vis a vis the new plans."

Translation: "We need to discuss the situation in relation to the new plans."

Explanation: A French term meaning "in relation to," used to compare or contrast things.

19. **Victory lap**

    Example: "He took a victory lap after winning the match."

    Translation: "He celebrated his victory after winning the match."

    Explanation: Refers to someone taking a celebratory moment after achieving success.

20. **Vicariously**

    Example: "I'm living vicariously through your adventures."

    Translation: "I'm enjoying your adventures as though I were experiencing them myself."

    Explanation: Refers to experiencing something indirectly, through someone else's experiences.

W

1. **Whinge**
   Example: "Stop whinging and get on with it!"
   Translation: "Stop complaining and get on with it!"
   Explanation: Refers to whining or complaining about something in a constant or annoying way.

2. **Wicked**
   Example: "That was a wicked surf session!"
   Translation: "That was an amazing surf session!"
   Explanation: Used to describe something that is really impressive, cool, or exciting.

3. **Woop woop**
   Example: "They live way out in woop woop, far from the city."
   Translation: "They live in a very remote area, far from the city."
   Explanation: A term used to describe a very remote or isolated place.

4. **Wag**
   Example: "I'm wagging school today to hang out with mates."
   Translation: "I'm skipping school today to hang out with friends."
   Explanation: Refers to skipping school or work without permission.

5. **Whack**
   Example: "That was a massive whack to the head!"
   Translation: "That was a big hit to the head!"

Explanation: Used to describe a heavy blow or impact.

6. **Wobble**

    Example: "She was nervous and her hands were wobbling."

    Translation: "She was nervous and her hands were shaking."

    Explanation: Refers to something that shakes or moves unsteadily.

7. **What a ripper!**

    Example: "The party last night was what a ripper!"

    Translation: "The party last night was fantastic!"

    Explanation: Used to describe something that is excellent or fantastic.

8. **Wild**

    Example: "That's a wild idea, but I love it!"

    Translation: "That's a crazy idea, but I love it!"

    Explanation: Refers to something unconventional, unexpected, or out of the ordinary.

9. **Walkabout**

    Example: "He's gone on walkabout for a few weeks to clear his head."

    Translation: "He's gone on a journey or trip to clear his head."

    Explanation: Refers to taking a journey, often to clear one's mind or explore nature.

10. **Wanna**

    Example: "Wanna grab a coffee later?"

    Translation: "Do you want to grab a coffee later?"

    Explanation: Informal contraction of "want to."

11. **Wuss**
    Example: "Come on, don't be such a wuss, it's just a joke!"
    Translation: "Come on, don't be such a coward, it's just a joke!"
    Explanation: Used to describe someone who is being overly fearful or weak in the face of something minor.
12. **Wasted**
    Example: "He was completely wasted at the party last night."
    Translation: "He was very drunk at the party last night."
    Explanation: Used to describe someone who is heavily intoxicated.
13. **Wind up**
    Example: "The boss is going to wind up the meeting now."
    Translation: "The boss is going to end the meeting now."
    Explanation: Refers to finishing something or bringing it to a close.
14. **Wacko**
    Example: "That was a wacko idea, but it worked!"
    Translation: "That was a crazy idea, but it worked!"
    Explanation: Used to describe something that is unusual, crazy, or unexpected.
15. **Waddle**
    Example: "The penguins waddle when they walk."
    Translation: "The penguins walk with a swaying motion."
    Explanation: Refers to walking with a short,

swaying gait, often used to describe penguins or someone walking awkwardly.

16. **Whizz**

    Example: "I need to have a whizz before we leave."

    Translation: "I need to go to the toilet before we leave."

    Explanation: Informal term for urinating.

17. **Wink**

    Example: "She gave him a cheeky wink across the room."

    Translation: "She gave him a playful wink across the room."

    Explanation: A gesture made by closing one eye briefly, often used to convey a secret message or flirtation.

18. **Welfare check**

    Example: "The police did a welfare check after her family couldn't reach her."

    Translation: "The police checked on her well-being after her family couldn't contact her."

    Explanation: A term for a safety check, especially when someone is not heard from or is in distress.

19. **White as a ghost**

    Example: "You're white as a ghost, are you alright?"

    Translation: "You look very pale, are you okay?"

    Explanation: Used to describe someone who appears pale due to shock, illness, or fear.

20. **Waddle on**

    Example: "Stop complaining and just waddle on with it!"

    Translation: "Stop complaining and keep

going with it!"
Explanation: Used in a playful sense to encourage someone to continue, even when they might be reluctant.

X

1. **Xanadu**
   Example: "This holiday house is like Xanadu, it's perfect!"
   Translation: "This holiday house is like paradise, it's perfect!"
   Explanation: Refers to an idealized, beautiful, or luxurious place, inspired by the legendary palace of the same name.
2. **X-factor**
   Example: "She's got the X-factor, no wonder she's a star!"
   Translation: "She has a special quality or talent that makes her stand out."
   Explanation: Refers to a special, unique quality that makes someone or something stand out or be successful.
3. **X-tra**
   Example: "That party was X-tra fun, we stayed out all night!"
   Translation: "That party was extra fun, we stayed out all night!"
   Explanation: Slang version of "extra," meaning something that is over the top or above what's expected.
4. **Xenial**
   Example: "He's a really xenial host, always making people feel welcome."
   Translation: "He's a really hospitable host, always making people feel welcome."
   Explanation: Refers to being hospitable or friendly to guests or strangers.

5. **Xenophobia**
   Example: "His xenophobia made him uncomfortable around tourists."
   Translation: "His fear or dislike of foreigners made him uncomfortable around tourists."
   Explanation: Refers to the fear or dislike of people from other countries.
6. **X-rated**
   Example: "That movie was X-rated, I couldn't believe how much swearing there was!"
   Translation: "That movie was rated for adults only, it had a lot of inappropriate language."
   Explanation: Refers to something that is explicit, particularly in reference to films with adult content.
7. **Xmas**
   Example: "Are you coming over for Xmas dinner?"
   Translation: "Are you coming over for Christmas dinner?"
   Explanation: Informal abbreviation for Christmas.
8. **X-cellent**
   Example: "That was an X-cellent performance, you nailed it!"
   Translation: "That was an excellent performance, you nailed it!"
   Explanation: A playful variation of "excellent," used to emphasize something done very well.
9. **Xenon lights**
   Example: "I installed xenon lights in my car, they're much brighter at night."
   Translation: "I installed xenon lights in my car, they provide brighter lighting at night."
   Explanation: Refers to a type of bright car

headlights, often used for their effectiveness in low-light conditions.

10. **Xplosive**

    Example: "The new album is absolutely xplosive, you have to listen to it!"

    Translation: "The new album is absolutely explosive, you have to listen to it!"

    Explanation: Refers to something that is very intense, energetic, or dramatic.

11. **Xmas party**

    Example: "Our work Xmas party is next Friday."

    Translation: "Our work Christmas party is next Friday."

    Explanation: Refers to a festive celebration for employees or friends during the Christmas season.

12. **X-tra mile**

    Example: "She went the x-tra mile to help with the charity event."

    Translation: "She went the extra mile to help with the charity event."

    Explanation: Refers to putting in additional effort beyond what is required.

13. **X-treme**

    Example: "He loves x-treme sports, always skydiving or surfing big waves."

    Translation: "He loves extreme sports, always skydiving or surfing big waves."

    Explanation: Refers to activities that are thrilling, risky, and out of the ordinary.

14. **Xenoglossy**

    Example: "She was speaking fluent French, though she had never studied it—some call it xenoglossy."

Translation: "She was speaking fluent French, though she had never studied it—some call it the phenomenon of speaking a language without having learned it."

Explanation: Refers to the phenomenon of speaking or understanding a language without having learned it.

15. **Xmas cheer**

    Example: "Everyone brought some Xmas cheer to the office with decorations."

    Translation: "Everyone brought some Christmas spirit to the office with decorations."

    Explanation: Refers to the joyful and festive atmosphere associated with Christmas celebrations.

16. **X-factors**

    Example: "The team's success was due to their x-factors, everyone brought something unique."

    Translation: "The team's success was due to their special qualities, everyone brought something unique."

    Explanation: Refers to the unique or special qualities that contribute to success.

17. **Xena warrior princess**

    Example: "She's a total Xena warrior princess—tough and determined!"

    Translation: "She's very tough and determined, like the character Xena from the show."

    Explanation: Refers to someone who is strong, independent, and capable of handling challenges, inspired by the popular TV character.

18. **X-tra chill**
    Example: "That beach day was x-tra chill, just lying around and relaxing."
    Translation: "That beach day was extremely relaxing, just lying around and taking it easy."
    Explanation: Refers to a highly relaxed or calm atmosphere.
19. **X-actly**
    Example: "X-actly, that's what I've been saying!"
    Translation: "Exactly, that's what I've been saying!"
    Explanation: A playful, emphatic version of "exactly," often used to express agreement.
20. **Xeno-**
    Example: "He had a real xeno-approach, trying to understand different cultures."
    Translation: "He had a real open-minded approach, trying to understand different cultures."
    Explanation: Prefix referring to foreign or unfamiliar things, often used in discussions of different cultures or experiences.

Y

1. **Yarn**
   Example: "We had a good yarn over coffee this morning."
   Translation: "We had a good conversation over coffee this morning."
   Explanation: Refers to a chat or informal conversation, often long and friendly.

2. **Yobbo**
   Example: "He's a total yobbo, always causing trouble at the pub."
   Translation: "He's a total lout, always causing trouble at the pub."
   Explanation: A derogatory term for a loud, uncouth, or unruly person.

3. **Yakka**
   Example: "I've been doing hard yakka all day!"
   Translation: "I've been working hard all day!"
   Explanation: Refers to hard physical labor or strenuous work.

4. **Yum**
   Example: "That chocolate cake looks yum!"
   Translation: "That chocolate cake looks delicious!"
   Explanation: An expression used to describe food that looks or tastes great.

5. **Yikes**
   Example: "Yikes, that was a close call!"
   Translation: "Wow, that was a close call!"
   Explanation: An exclamation of surprise or shock, often in response to something unexpected or alarming.

6. **Yobbo**
   Example: "The yobbo next door is always

blaring his music."
Translation: "The rowdy guy next door is always blaring his music."
Explanation: A term for a noisy, rowdy person, often with a connotation of rudeness or lack of sophistication.

7. **Yup**
   Example: "You coming to the party tonight?" "Yup, I'll be there!"
   Translation: "You coming to the party tonight?" "Yes, I'll be there!"
   Explanation: Informal, enthusiastic affirmative response to a question.

8. **Yowie**
   Example: "They say the yowie lives deep in the Australian outback."
   Translation: "They say the mythical creature, the yowie, lives deep in the Australian outback."
   Explanation: A creature from Australian folklore, similar to Bigfoot, said to inhabit remote parts of the country.

9. **Yellow-bellied**
   Example: "He's too yellow-bellied to stand up for himself."
   Translation: "He's too cowardly to stand up for himself."
   Explanation: A term used to describe someone as being cowardly or lacking bravery.

10. **Yank**
    Example: "That's a classic yank move!"
    Translation: "That's a classic American move!"
    Explanation: A colloquial term for an American person, often used in a humorous or light-hearted way.

11. **Yob**
    Example: "Don't be such a yob, mate!"
    Translation: "Don't be such a jerk, mate!"
    Explanation: Another version of "yobbo," meaning a rude or loutish person.
12. **Yippee**
    Example: "Yippee, it's the weekend!"
    Translation: "Hooray, it's the weekend!"
    Explanation: An exclamation used to express excitement or happiness.
13. **You beauty!**
    Example: "We won the game! You beauty!"
    Translation: "We won the game! How awesome!"
    Explanation: A celebratory exclamation used to express excitement or approval.
14. **Yonder**
    Example: "They live over yonder, near the coast."
    Translation: "They live over there, near the coast."
    Explanation: An old-fashioned or poetic term referring to a distant location.
15. **Yobbo barbie**
    Example: "We're having a yobbo barbie at my place this weekend!"
    Translation: "We're having a casual BBQ at my place this weekend!"
    Explanation: A casual, laid-back BBQ or party, often involving a lot of drinking and loud behavior.
16. **Yuppie**
    Example: "She's a bit of a yuppie, always working in the city and buying expensive clothes."

Translation: "She's a young urban professional, always working in the city and buying expensive clothes."
Explanation: Refers to a young, ambitious, and typically well-off person, often with a focus on career and material wealth.

17. **Yanked**
    Example: "He got yanked out of the party for causing trouble."
    Translation: "He got pulled out of the party for causing trouble."
    Explanation: A term meaning to be forcibly removed or taken away.

18. **Yardie**
    Example: "Those yardies are running the street corner now."
    Translation: "The people from the local Jamaican community are now in control of the street corner."
    Explanation: Refers to a member of a particular Caribbean or Jamaican community, often in a context of street culture or gangs.

19. **Yellow card**
    Example: "The ref showed him a yellow card for his bad tackle."
    Translation: "The referee gave him a warning for his foul tackle."
    Explanation: A term used in sports, particularly soccer, referring to a warning given by the referee for unsporting behavior.

20. **Yakkity yak**
    Example: "All he does is yakkity yak about his new car."
    Translation: "All he does is talk endlessly about his new car."

Explanation: Refers to excessive talking, often without saying anything of real importance.

Z

1. **Zonked**
   Example: "I'm completely zonked after that big hike!"
   Translation: "I'm completely exhausted after that big hike!"
   Explanation: A term used to describe feeling extremely tired or worn out.

2. **Zebra Crossing**
   Example: "I almost got hit while crossing at the zebra crossing."
   Translation: "I almost got hit while crossing at the pedestrian crosswalk."
   Explanation: Refers to a pedestrian crossing marked with white stripes, commonly called a "zebra crossing."

3. **Zero to Hero**
   Example: "He went from zero to hero after scoring the winning goal."
   Translation: "He went from being unnoticed to being celebrated after scoring the winning goal."
   Explanation: Refers to a dramatic transformation, often from failure or obscurity to success or fame.

4. **Zinger**
   Example: "She came out with a real zinger of a joke!"
   Translation: "She came out with a really funny or clever joke!"
   Explanation: A witty or humorous remark that has an impact, often one that surprises or impresses.

5. **Zip it**
   Example: "Zip it, mate, you're talking too much!"
   Translation: "Be quiet, mate, you're talking too much!"
   Explanation: A slang expression telling someone to stop talking, similar to saying "shut up."
6. **Zapped**
   Example: "After working all day, I'm completely zapped."
   Translation: "After working all day, I'm completely drained."
   Explanation: Refers to being completely exhausted or depleted of energy.
7. **Zebra**
   Example: "That new dress is a real zebra, isn't it?"
   Translation: "That new dress is really eye-catching and unique, isn't it?"
   Explanation: A term for something that stands out or is particularly striking, often with black-and-white colors.
8. **Zonked out**
   Example: "He zonked out on the couch after the long day at work."
   Translation: "He passed out on the couch after the long day at work."
   Explanation: A slang term for falling asleep or passing out due to exhaustion.
9. **Zip-a-dee-doo-dah**
   Example: "She was humming 'zip-a-dee-doo-dah' all day, feeling so happy."
   Translation: "She was humming a cheerful song all day, feeling so happy."

Explanation: An upbeat, cheerful song or phrase often associated with being in a good mood.

10. **Zapped out**
Example: "I feel completely zapped out after the gym session."
Translation: "I feel completely drained after the gym session."
Explanation: Another variation of being mentally or physically exhausted.

11. **Zig-zag**
Example: "We had to zig-zag through the crowd to find our seats."
Translation: "We had to weave through the crowd to find our seats."
Explanation: Refers to a pattern of movement that alternates direction in sharp turns, often used to describe moving through obstacles.

12. **Zinger of a comeback**
Example: "She made a zinger of a comeback during the debate!"
Translation: "She made a really sharp and effective response during the debate!"
Explanation: Refers to a quick, clever, and impactful comeback in conversation or argument.

13. **Zipline**
Example: "We went ziplining over the rainforest—what a rush!"
Translation: "We went ziplining over the rainforest—what an exciting experience!"
Explanation: A recreational activity where you ride a cable from a high point to a lower one, typically in a thrilling outdoor setting.

14. **Zombie mode**
    Example: "I'm in zombie mode this morning, I didn't sleep well last night."
    Translation: "I'm feeling sluggish and exhausted this morning, I didn't sleep well last night."
    Explanation: Refers to a state of being tired or mentally drained, often appearing like a "zombie."
15. **Zero chill**
    Example: "She had zero chill when she found out she didn't get the job."
    Translation: "She had no composure or calmness when she found out she didn't get the job."
    Explanation: Refers to a person who reacts in an overly emotional or dramatic way, without the ability to stay calm.
16. **Zebra stripes**
    Example: "I love the zebra stripes on that dress!"
    Translation: "I love the black-and-white striped pattern on that dress!"
    Explanation: Refers to a bold pattern of alternating black and white stripes.
17. **Zappy**
    Example: "I feel so zappy today—ready to take on anything!"
    Translation: "I feel so energetic today—ready to take on anything!"
    Explanation: A playful term to describe feeling lively, full of energy, or excited.
18. **Zoning out**
    Example: "I was zoning out during that long lecture."

Translation: "I was mentally drifting off and not paying attention during that long lecture."
Explanation: Refers to becoming distracted or mentally disengaged, usually when someone isn't focusing on the present situation.

19. **Zoomer**
Example: "That guy's a real zoomer on the skatepark, always pulling off sick tricks."
Translation: "That guy's a real pro on the skatepark, always pulling off impressive tricks."
Explanation: A term used to refer to someone who is fast, skilled, or energetic, often used in the context of sports or physical activities.

20. **Zipped up**
Example: "She's all zipped up in her jacket, ready to go!"
Translation: "She's fully dressed and ready to go, her jacket is zipped up!"
Explanation: Refers to being prepared or dressed warmly, with a focus on the zippered clothing item.

Printed in Great Britain
by Amazon